הַגָּדָה שֶׁל פֶּסַח

The Family Participation Haggadah

A DIFFERENT NIGHT

By Noam Zion and David Dishon

The complete Passover text with educational innovations to involve everyone at the Seder – adult and child alike.

with illustrations by Tanya Zion, Ben Shahn, Otto Geismar and many others

מכון
שלום
הרטמן
SHALOM HARTMAN INSTITUTE • JERUSALEM, ISRAEL

The David and Rae Finegood Institute for Diaspora Education
The Charles and Valerie Diker Family Resource Center for Jewish Continuity

> "The real question is not why do we keep Passover but how do we continue to keep Passover year after year and keep it from becoming stultified!
> How can we be privileged to plan it so that, as Rabbi Abraham Isaac Kook said, *The old may become new and the new may become holy.*"
>
> IRA STEINGROOT

> "One must make changes on this night, so the children will notice and ask: *Why is this night different?*"
>
> MAIMONIDES

> "Only the lesson which is enjoyed can be learned well."
>
> JUDAH HANASI

1

Table of Contents

Introduction

First Cup: Kiddush

From Slavery to Freedom   *Otto Geismar, 1927*

Second Cup: Storytelling

Table of Contents continued

Shortcuts Through the Haggadah

This Haggadah offers resources for many years of Pesach Seders. Pick and choose the readings and activities that are most appropriate for the Seder at hand. If you are pressed for time, follow our non-traditional **"Bare Bones Basic Seder"** which hits all the highlights and still leaves time to try some new ideas.

Bare Bones Basic Seder: pp. 8, 10, 12, 14, 16, 18, 20, 22, (35-36), 46, 48, 52-54, 57-60, 62-63, (65), 68, 85. But don't miss the extras: The Art of the Four Children (pp. 24-33) and the songs (pp. 75-84).

Can you find how many cartoon illustrations of the afikoman/matza are dispersed throughout the Haggadah?

Candle Lighting

הַדְלָקַת נֵרוֹת

1. **Lighting the candles** marks the beginning of Pesach as well as the end of the frantic work of preparation. It contributes to the transition to sanctity.

2. **Before sunset**, it is traditional to light at least two candles placed on or near the table. Some families light one candle for each family member. Others prepare two candles for each woman over the age of bat mitzvah. Ideally, the candles should be longer lasting than usual, so they will provide light for the length of the Seder.

3. **Usually on Pesach** one first recites the blessing and then lights the candles without covering one's eyes. However, when Seder night occurs on Friday night, then one lights the candles first, covers one's eyes and then recites the blessing.

BLESSED ARE YOU, Adonai our God, Ruler of the Universe, who sanctified us by commanding us to light the [Shabbat and] holiday candles.

Many say the following when lighting the candles, while others recite it together with Kiddush (There is no need to recite this blessing twice).

BLESSED ARE YOU, Adonai our God, Ruler of the Universe, who has kept us alive and brought us to this happy moment in our lives.

Ba-ruch ata Adonai,
Elo-hei-nu me-lech ha-olam,
asher kee-d'sha-nu b'meetz-vo-tav
v'tzee-va-nu l'had-leek ner shel
[Shabbat v'shel] Yom Tov.

Ba-ruch ata Adonai,
Elo-hei-nu me-lech ha-olam
she-he-chee-ya-nu v'kee-ma-nu
v'hee-gee-anu laz-man ha-ze.

בָּרוּךְ אַתָּה יְיָ אֱלֹהֵינוּ מֶלֶךְ
הָעוֹלָם, אֲשֶׁר קִדְּשָׁנוּ
בְּמִצְוֹתָיו, וְצִוָּנוּ לְהַדְלִיק נֵר
שֶׁל (שַׁבָּת וְשֶׁל) יוֹם טוֹב.

בָּרוּךְ אַתָּה יְיָ,
אֱלֹהֵינוּ מֶלֶךְ הָעוֹלָם,
שֶׁהֶחֱיָנוּ וְקִיְּמָנוּ
וְהִגִּיעָנוּ לַזְּמַן הַזֶּה.

A Traditional Woman's Prayer at Candle Lighting

May it be Your will, God of our ancestors, that You grant my family and all Israel a good and long life. Remember us with blessings and kindness, fill our home with your Divine Presence. Give me the opportunity to raise my children and grandchildren to be truly wise, lovers of God, people of truth, who illuminate the world with Torah, good deeds and the work of the Creator. Please hear my prayer at this time. Regard me as a worthy descendant of Sarah, Rebecca, Rachel and Leah, our mothers, and let my candles burn and never be extinguished. Let the light of your face shine upon us. Amen.

Blessing the Children

בִּרְכַּת יְלָדִים

The custom of blessing one's offspring originates with Jacob and his grandchildren. On the eve of Yom Kippur, on Shabbat and holidays many parents lay their hands on the head of each child, blessing them with the priests' benediction.

A Private Moment of Intimacy with our Children

Rabbi Jacob Emden of Prague (19th c.) recommends that one place both hands on the child's head, just as Moshe blessed Joshua his successor with two hands – without reservation, without jealousy. The priests also bless the people with two open-faced hands as an expression of love. "Everyone can also take this opportunity to add their own personal blessing to each child according to one's gift of eloquence" (Siddur Bet El). There are only two lasting bequests we can hope to give our children. One of these is **roots**; the other, **wings**.

For male children:

MAY GOD make you like Ephraim and Menashe.

יְשִׂימְךָ אֱלֹהִים כְּאֶפְרַיִם וְכִמְנַשֶּׁה.

(Genesis 48:20 from Jacob's blessing for his grandchildren)

For female children:

MAY GOD make you like Sarah and Rebecca, Rachel and Leah.

יְשִׂימֵךְ אֱלֹהִים כְּשָׂרָה רִבְקָה רָחֵל וְלֵאָה.

(See Ruth 4:11, the women's blessing for Ruth the convert)

For all:

MAY GOD bless you and keep you.
May God's face shine upon you and favor you.
May God's face turn to you
and grant you shalom.

יְבָרֶכְךָ יְיָ וְיִשְׁמְרֶךָ
יָאֵר יְיָ פָּנָיו אֵלֶיךָ וִיחֻנֶּךָּ
יִשָּׂא יְיָ פָּנָיו אֵלֶיךָ
וְיָשֵׂם לְךָ שָׁלוֹם.

(Numbers 6:24-26, the priestly benediction)

WHO IS GOD?*WELL IT IS AN INVISIBLE PERSON AND HE LIVES UP IN HEAVEN* I GUESS UP IN OUTER SPACE*HE MADE THE EARTH AND THE HEAVEN & THE STARS AND THE SUN AND THE PEOPLE*HE MADE LIGHT HE MADE DAY HE MADE NIGHT*HE HAS SUCH POWERFUL EYES HE DOESN'T HAVE MILLIONS AND THOUSANDS AND BILLIONS AND HE CAN STILL SEE US WHEN WE'RE BAD* HE STARTED ALL THE PLANTS GROWING*TO ME I THINK OF HIM WHO MAKES FLOWERS & GREEN GRASS & THE BLUE SKY & THE YELLOW SUN*GOD IS EVERYWHERE & I DON'T KNOW HOW HE COULD DO IT

Who Knows God?

Ben Shahn © 1996 Ben Shahn Estate Licensed by VAGA, NY, NY

Signposts for the Seder

סִימָנֵי הַסֵּדֶר

1. **The official opening** of the Seder should begin by welcoming all the guests. Make sure to introduce all the participants, so that everyone will be made to feel part of the Jewish family – especially on a night when we recall what it felt like to be strangers in the land of Egypt. You may ask all the participants to say their Hebrew names as well.

2. **We review** briefly the order of the Seder by singing the medieval poem by Rabbenu Shmuel of Falaise (France) that summarizes the Signposts of the Seder ("Kadesh Urchatz").

3. **You may wish** to give credit to all who have helped prepare this Seder – its foods, its readings and its activities.

THE 15 STEPS OF THE SEDER

All sing:	**Kadesh**	First cup and Kiddush	קַדֵּשׁ וּרְחַץ
	UrChatz	First handwashing (without a blessing)	
	Karpas	First dipping: vegetable and salt water	כַּרְפַּס יַחַץ
	Yachatz	Breaking the middle matza	
	Maggid	Storytelling	מַגִּיד רַחְצָה
	Rachtza	Second handwashing (with a blessing)	
	Motzi	First blessing over the matza	מוֹצִיא מַצָּה
	Matza	Second blessing over the matza	
	Maror	Second dipping: maror in charoset.	מָרוֹר כּוֹרֵךְ
	Korech	Hillel sandwich	
	Shulchan Orech	Festive meal	שֻׁלְחָן עוֹרֵךְ
	Tzafun	Afikoman (dessert)	צָפוּן בָּרֵךְ
	Barech	Birkat hamazon (the blessing after eating)	
	Hallel	Psalms of praise	הַלֵּל נִרְצָה
	Nirtza	Concluding prayer and folk songs	

Kadesh: Sanctifying Time
Kiddush

קַדֵּשׁ

1. **The Kiddush** sanctifies not the wine, but the holiday. Pesach is dedicated to – "Remember the **Day of your Exodus from Egypt**" (Ex.13:3). (On Shabbat we add the texts in shaded boxes and in parentheses in the body of the Kiddush to commemorate the Creation of the World).

2. **Offer to pour** the wine or grape juice into someone else's cup. In turn each one is served by another as befits royalty. Having attained the high status of freedom we celebrate it in style, preferably with red wine, because the rabbis considered it more elegant.

3. **Stand** to recite the Kiddush, then **recline** to the left to drink the wine, as befits Greco-Roman nobles who also reclined to the left at symposia (intellectual drinking banquets). If there are no pillows on the chairs, ask the children to bring as many as possible.

הִנְנִי מוּכָן וּמְזֻמָּן לְקַיֵּם מִצְוַת כּוֹס רִאשׁוֹן
שֶׁל אַרְבַּע כּוֹסוֹת.

HERE I AM, ready to perform the mitzvah of the first cup of wine and to dedicate this whole evening "to telling the story of wonders performed for our ancestors on the night of the 15th of Nisan," 3,200 years ago. *(Maimonides, Chametz 7:1).*

"Don't Cry over Spilt Wine"

A PUBLIC MESSAGE from the Hosts to All Their Guests:"Don't Cry over Spilt Wine."

Rabbi Akiba Eiger *(Germany, 18th C.)* used to be very strict about the mitzvah of hospitality especially on Pesach. Once when he was leading a large Seder, one of the guests happened to spill a cup of wine. The clean white tablecloth was stained. Seeing the guest's enormous embarrassment, Rabbi Eiger himself bumped the table spilling his own glass of wine. He exclaimed: "**Oh, this table must be off-balance.**"

On Shabbat rise and recite from Genesis 2:1-3:

[There was evening and there was morning, and the sixth day was over. The sky and the earth and all their contents were completed. On the seventh day God completed all the work. God ceased (*shabbat*) from all activity. God blessed the seventh day and declared it holy, because on that day God ceased from all the work of creation.]

(וַיְהִי עֶרֶב וַיְהִי בֹקֶר)
יוֹם הַשִּׁשִּׁי, וַיְכֻלּוּ הַשָּׁמַיִם וְהָאָרֶץ וְכָל צְבָאָם. וַיְכַל אֱלֹהִים בַּיּוֹם
הַשְּׁבִיעִי, מְלַאכְתּוֹ אֲשֶׁר עָשָׂה, וַיִּשְׁבֹּת בַּיּוֹם הַשְּׁבִיעִי, מִכָּל
מְלַאכְתּוֹ אֲשֶׁר עָשָׂה. וַיְבָרֶךְ אֱלֹהִים אֶת יוֹם הַשְּׁבִיעִי, וַיְקַדֵּשׁ אֹתוֹ,
כִּי בוֹ שָׁבַת מִכָּל מְלַאכְתּוֹ, אֲשֶׁר בָּרָא אֱלֹהִים לַעֲשׂוֹת.

BLESSED ARE YOU, Adonai
our God, Ruler of the Universe,
who creates the fruit of the vine.

Ba-ruch ata Adonai,
Elo-hei-nu me-lech ha-olam,
bo-rei pree ha-gafen.

בָּרוּךְ אַתָּה יְיָ,
אֱלֹהֵינוּ מֶלֶךְ הָעוֹלָם,
בּוֹרֵא פְּרִי הַגָּפֶן.

BLESSED ARE YOU, Adonai our God, Ruler of the
Universe, who has chosen us from among the nations
and the languages, sanctifying us by your mitzvot.
Lovingly, You have given us [Shabbat for rest and] **festivals
for happiness**, including today –
[the Shabbat and] the **Holiday of the
Matzot**, the **season of our liberation**,
a sacred day to gather together and to
commemorate the Exodus from
Egypt. For You have chosen us and
sanctified us among the nations.
You have granted us [lovingly the
Shabbat and] joyfully the
holidays. Blessed are You,
Adonai, who sanctifies [the
Shabbat and] the people of
Israel and the festivals.

בָּרוּךְ אַתָּה יְיָ, אֱלֹהֵינוּ מֶלֶךְ הָעוֹלָם, אֲשֶׁר בָּחַר בָּנוּ
מִכָּל עָם, וְרוֹמְמָנוּ מִכָּל לָשׁוֹן, וְקִדְּשָׁנוּ בְּמִצְוֹתָיו,
וַתִּתֶּן לָנוּ יְיָ אֱלֹהֵינוּ בְּאַהֲבָה (שַׁבָּתוֹת לִמְנוּחָה וּ)מוֹעֲדִים
לְשִׂמְחָה, חַגִּים וּזְמַנִּים לְשָׂשׂוֹן אֶת יוֹם (הַשַּׁבָּת הַזֶּה
וְאֶת יוֹם) חַג הַמַּצּוֹת הַזֶּה, זְמַן חֵרוּתֵנוּ, (בְּאַהֲבָה),
מִקְרָא קֹדֶשׁ, זֵכֶר לִיצִיאַת מִצְרָיִם. כִּי בָנוּ
בָחַרְתָּ וְאוֹתָנוּ קִדַּשְׁתָּ מִכָּל הָעַמִּים.
(וְשַׁבָּת) וּמוֹעֲדֵי קָדְשֶׁךָ (בְּאַהֲבָה וּבְרָצוֹן)
בְּשִׂמְחָה וּבְשָׂשׂוֹן הִנְחַלְתָּנוּ.
בָּרוּךְ אַתָּה יְיָ, מְקַדֵּשׁ
(הַשַּׁבָּת וְ)יִשְׂרָאֵל
וְהַזְּמַנִּים.

*On Saturday night
only, insert Havdalah
here (page 9) before
Shehecheeyanu.*

BLESSED ARE YOU,
Adonai our God, Ruler
of the Universe, who
has kept us alive and
brought us to this happy
moment in our lives.

בָּרוּךְ אַתָּה יְיָ,
אֱלֹהֵינוּ מֶלֶךְ הָעוֹלָם,
שֶׁהֶחֱיָנוּ וְקִיְּמָנוּ
וְהִגִּיעָנוּ לַזְּמַן הַזֶּה.

*Now be seated, recline com-
fortably leaning to the left on a
pillow, and drink most of the cup.*

Tully Filmus

Havdalah הַבְדָּלָה

On Saturday night:

Havdalah is the blessing over the distinction between Shabbat and the weekdays. The light of the fire is blessed using the festival candles already lit. (No special Havdalah candle or spice box are necessary):

[Blessed are You, Adonai our God, Ruler of the Universe, who creates the lights of fire.

Blessed are You, Adonai our God, Ruler of the Universe, who **differentiates** between the holy and the secular, between light and darkness, between Israel and the other nations, between the seventh day and the six days of creation, between the sanctity of Shabbat and the sanctity of Yom Tov (the festivals). You sanctified the people of Israel with Your holiness.

Blessed are You, Adonai, who **differentiates** between the holiness of Shabbat and the holiness of Yom Tov.]

בָּרוּךְ אַתָּה יְיָ, אֱלֹהֵינוּ מֶלֶךְ הָעוֹלָם, בּוֹרֵא מְאוֹרֵי הָאֵשׁ.

בָּרוּךְ אַתָּה יְיָ, אֱלֹהֵינוּ מֶלֶךְ הָעוֹלָם, הַמַּבְדִּיל בֵּין קֹדֶשׁ לְחֹל בֵּין אוֹר לְחֹשֶׁךְ, בֵּין יִשְׂרָאֵל לָעַמִּים, בֵּין יוֹם הַשְּׁבִיעִי לְשֵׁשֶׁת יְמֵי הַמַּעֲשֶׂה. בֵּין קְדֻשַּׁת שַׁבָּת לִקְדֻשַּׁת יוֹם טוֹב הִבְדַּלְתָּ. וְאֶת יוֹם הַשְּׁבִיעִי מִשֵּׁשֶׁת יְמֵי הַמַּעֲשֶׂה קִדַּשְׁתָּ. הִבְדַּלְתָּ וְקִדַּשְׁתָּ אֶת עַמְּךָ יִשְׂרָאֵל בִּקְדֻשָּׁתֶךָ.

בָּרוּךְ אַתָּה יְיָ, הַמַּבְדִּיל בֵּין קֹדֶשׁ לְקֹדֶשׁ.

From Rags to Riches: A Folktale

IRAQI JEWS tell the tale that in one country the king was always chosen in a special way. When the old king died, a bird called the "bird of good fortune" would be released. On whomsoever's head it landed, the people would place the crown making him their next ruler.

Once the bird of good fortune landed on the head of a slave. That slave had been a simple musician who entertained at the master's parties. His costume consisted of a feathered cap and a belt made of the hooves of sheep.

When the slave became king, he moved into the palace and wore royal robes. However, he ordered that a shack (a kind of sukkah) be constructed next to the palace and that his old hat, belt and drum be stored there along with a giant mirror.

The new king was known for his kindness and love for all his people – rich and poor, free and slave. Often he would disappear into his little shack. Once he left its door open and the cabinet ministers saw him don his feathered hat, put on his old belt and dance and drum before the mirror. They found this very strange and asked the king:

"After all, you are a king! You must maintain your dignity!"

The king replied:

"Once I was a slave and now I've become a king. From time to time I want to remind myself that I was once a slave lest I grow arrogant and treat with disdain my people and you, my ministers."

(The English term, "auspicious day" or "inauguration day" preserves an echo of the Roman custom of consulting the flight of birds as an "augur" for the future).

Tanya Zion

Urchatz   *The First Handwashing*   יוּרְחַץ

1. **The ritual handwashing** *prepares us for eating finger foods, Karpas, the hors d'oeuvres of the Pesach banquet. It sanctifies the act of eating.*

2. **Ask for two volunteers:** *one to carry a pitcher of water and to pour water over each guest's hands, and one to carry a basin and a towel. No blessing is said for this handwashing.*

Karpas   *The First Dipping — Spring Greens*      כַּרְפַּס

1. **Distribute Karpas** *(a vegetable) and dip it in salt water, while reciting the appropriate blessing. Some Jews dip in charoset.*

2. **While some** *medieval rabbis strictly forbid eating more than an olive's size of parsley for Karpas, you may wish to* revive the ancient custom of eating **extensive appetizers** – *each with its own dip. You may continue dipping and tasting various fresh vegetables and other appetizers during the Seder until sufficiently full to persevere during the extensive story-telling (Maggid), but not so full as to ruin one's appetite for the matza eaten later.*

For vegetables (like celery, parsley, or potatoes):

BLESSED ARE YOU, Adonai our God, Ruler of the Universe, who creates the fruit of the earth.

Ba-ruch ata Adonai,
Elo-hei-nu me-lech ha-olam,
bo-rei pree ha-ada-ma.

בָּרוּךְ אַתָּה יְיָ,
אֱלֹהֵינוּ מֶלֶךְ הָעוֹלָם,
בּוֹרֵא פְּרִי הָאֲדָמָה.

Yachatz   *Breaking the Matza*   יַחַץ

1. **Breaking the Matza** *is one of many ritual acts that turn the food of the Seder into a symbol of meaning.*

2. **Count off** *the matzot from top to bottom: 1, 2, 3, naming them, if you wish, "Cohen," "Levi" and "Yisrael" (the three ritual classes of the Jewish people).*
   The top matza is for the usual blessing over bread (motzi). Tonight that blessing is recited over matza.
   The bottom matza is for the Hillel sandwich (korech) made with matza, maror, and charoset.

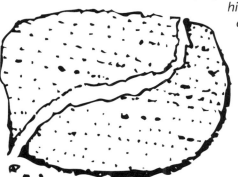

3. **Break the middle** *matza in two and explain that this is for a dual purpose: the bigger portion is to be hidden for the "afikoman" and eaten when retrieved from the children for dessert. It will be the last taste of food at the Seder. The smaller portion will be eaten with the top matza when we say the special blessing over matza at the beginning of the meal.*

10

The Story of the Compulsive Saver

IN THE JERUSALEM neighborhood of Talpiot lived an eccentric old man in a large villa. He visited the synagogue religiously whenever a kiddush was served with cakes and kugel. At shul everyone filled themselves with sweets but this elderly man took twice as much, filling his pockets and his mouth. His fellow Jews smiled at his anxious hoarding and wondered how a man living in a large house could be so desperate for a little cake.

Once a curious Jew asked him to explain. The old man replied heavily: "In the concentration camps in Poland there was never enough bread. I have never liberated myself from my fear that tomorrow there may not be any more food."

A Personal Thanksgiving

The Pesach family gathering is in fact a thanksgiving banquet during which we retell our national salvation. It is also appropriate to weave into the Seder, memories of personal deliverance from danger. Invite the family and guests to recall their own family stories of redemption from illness, from danger, or from persecution. Perhaps they can discuss the lessons they drew from these crucial events in their lives.

Pesach: The Spring Holiday.
Shraga Weil, Song of Songs © 1968

Why Karpas?

The word "Karpas" derives from the Greek "Karpos" meaning fruit of the soil. The historical origins of dipping Karpas at the Seder reflect the accepted cuisine of the Greco-Roman symposium.

Metaphorically, Karpas, the spring vegetable, represents both the historic birth of Israel out of the womb of Egypt and the rebirth of nature renewed each spring. According to Philo and to Rabbi Joshua the original birthday of nature – the Creation – occurred at Pesach-time, not Rosh Hashana. Similarly, the Italian name for spring *prima-vera* and the French *printemps* preserve the sense of the return to the original "first time" of the world.

Spring (old English) is originally applied to the place of origin from which a stream arises. Later it was applied to the season, the "spring of the year."

Maggid: Ha Lachma Anya

מַגִּיד הָא לַחְמָא עַנְיָא

Telling the Story: 'This is the Bread of Poverty and Persecution'

1. **The heart of the Seder** is "Maggid" from the term "Haggadah" meaning storytelling. In words but also in drama we retell the Exodus, beginning with an Aramaic explanation of the origin of matza.

2. **Remove** the cloth covering the matzot so that they are in plain view during the telling of the story, the Maggid. **Raise** the three matzot and point out the broken middle matza. Now the afikoman, the second half of the middle matza, is hidden until dessert.

3. **Some Rabbis** require the Seder plate as well as the matzot to be lifted up, as if they were about to be removed from the table even before the meal has begun. This was originally designed to arouse the children to ask questions.

4. Many Jews from **African-Asian countries** open the Maggid with a **Passover skit**. Experiment with the script (provided on p. 13). **Morrocan Jews** pass the matzot over everyone's head while reciting Ha Lachma Anya. Some people open the door at this point, as if to offer hospitality to anyone without a Seder.

Kadesh
Urchatz
Karpas
Yachatz
Maggid

Ha
Lachma
Anya

HA LACHMA ANYA

THIS IS THE BREAD of poverty and persecution that our ancestors ate in the land of Egypt. As it says in the Torah *"seven days shall you eat . . . matzot – the bread of poverty and persecution"* (Deut. 16:3) so that you may *"remember that you were a slave in Egypt . . ."* (Deut. 16:12).

LET ALL who are hungry, come and eat
LET ALL who are in need, come and share the Pesach meal.

THIS YEAR we are still here –
Next year, in the land of Israel.

THIS YEAR we are still slaves –
Next year, free people.

Ha la-ch-ma an-ya
Dee-acha-lu av-ha-ta-na
B'ar-ah d'meetz-ra-yeem.

Kol deech-feen, yei-tei v' yei-chol,
Kol dee-tzreech, yei-tei v' yee-fsach.

Ha-sha-ta ha-cha,
L'sha-na ha-ba-ah
be-ar-ah d'yis-rael

Ha-sha-ta av-dei,
L'sha-na ha-ba-ah
B'nei cho-reen.

הָא לַחְמָא עַנְיָא
דִּי אֲכָלוּ אַבְהָתָנָא
בְּאַרְעָא דְמִצְרָיִם.

כָּל דִּכְפִין יֵיתֵי וְיֵכֹל,
כָּל דִּצְרִיךְ יֵיתֵי וְיִפְסַח.

הָשַׁתָּא הָכָא,
לְשָׁנָה הַבָּאָה
בְּאַרְעָא דְיִשְׂרָאֵל.

הָשַׁתָּא עַבְדֵי,
לְשָׁנָה הַבָּאָה
בְּנֵי חוֹרִין.

A Passover Skit

In Egypt the Jews ate quickly and anxiously because they were nervous about the plague of the first born and they were expecting their imminent departure into freedom. Today Jews of Africa and Asia customarily act out the Exodus itself dressing their children (or a dramatically inclined adult) in baggy clothes, a scarf or hat, hiking boots, a walking stick, a belt with a canteen and, most important, the afikoman wrapped in one's clothes on the shoulder (or perhaps in a back pack).

Try sending the youngest children out of the room (or the house) with a bag of props and the help of an adult to prepare this dialogue. Here is a semi-traditional script that may be used by the "actors" at the Seder.

An Open Door Policy

BEFORE COMMENCING any meal, Rav Huna of Babylonia used to **open** the door and announce: "Let all who are in need come and eat" (B.T. Taanit 20b).

Concern for the needy is characteristic of every Jewish celebration. The Torah emphasizes: "*You shall rejoice in your festival – with your son and daughter, your male and female servant, the Levi, the stranger, the orphan and the widow in your communities*" (Deut. 16:14).

Knock on the door

Adults - Who's there?

Children - Moshe, Aaron, and Miriam.

Adults - Come in. Tell us about your journey!

Children - We have just arrived from Egypt where we were slaves to Pharaoh. He made us do such hard work. [*Improvise about how bad it was.*]

Adults - How did you escape?

Children - God sent Moshe and Aaron to tell Pharaoh: "Let my people go." When he refused, God sent 10 plagues. [*Improvise describing some of the plagues.*] Finally God brought the most awful plague on the first born of Egypt. Then Pharaoh was really scared, so he kicked us out.

Adults - Why are you dressed like that? What is on your shoulder?

Prague, 1526

Children - We escaped in the middle of the night and had no time to let the dough for our bread rise. The dough that we wrapped in our cloaks and slung over our shoulders turned to matza in the heat of the sun.

Adults - Tell us about your adventures.

Children - Pharaoh changed his mind after releasing us and chased us to the edge of the Red Sea. We would have been caught for sure, but then God split the sea. [*Describe how it felt.*]

Adults - Where are you going now?

Children - To Jerusalem.

All - **La-shana ha-ba-ah Bee'Yerushalayeem!**

Four Questions

1. **Pour** the second cup for everyone and let the younger children sing "Ma Nishtana."

מַה נִּשְׁתַּנָּה

2. Some people distribute nuts and candies to reward the children's curiosity.

Kadesh
Urchatz
Karpas
Yachatz
Maggid

Four
Questions

MA NISHTANA

מַה נִּשְׁתַּנָּה

HOW IS THIS NIGHT different
from all other nights?

Ma nish-ta-na ha-lai-la ha-zeh,
mee-kol ha-lei-lot?

הַלַּיְלָה הַזֶּה
מִכָּל הַלֵּילוֹת?

ON ALL other nights,
we eat
either leavened bread or matza,
but on this night we eat only **matza**.

She-b'chol ha-lei-lot,
anu och-leen,
cha-metz u-matza
Ha-lai-la ha-zeh, ku-lo matza.

שֶׁבְּכָל הַלֵּילוֹת
אָנוּ אוֹכְלִין
חָמֵץ וּמַצָּה,
הַלַּיְלָה הַזֶּה כֻּלּוֹ מַצָּה.

ON ALL other nights,
we eat other kinds of vegetables,
but on this night we eat **maror** (bitter herbs).

She-b'chol ha-lei-lot
anu och-leen sh'ar y'ra-kot,
Ha-lai-la ha-zeh maror.

שֶׁבְּכָל הַלֵּילוֹת
אָנוּ אוֹכְלִין שְׁאָר יְרָקוֹת
הַלַּיְלָה הַזֶּה מָרוֹר.

ON ALL other nights,
we need not dip
our vegetables even once,
but on this night we **dip** twice.

She-b'chol ha-lei-lot
ein anu mat-bee-leen,
afee-lu pa-am achat
Ha-lai-la ha-zeh, shtei-p'ameem.

שֶׁבְּכָל הַלֵּילוֹת
אֵין אָנוּ מַטְבִּילִין
אֲפִילוּ פַּעַם אֶחָת,
הַלַּיְלָה הַזֶּה שְׁתֵּי פְעָמִים.

ON ALL other nights,
we eat
either sitting upright
or reclining,
but on this night
we all **recline**.

She-b'chol ha-lei-lot
anu och-leen,
bein yo-shveen
u-vein m'su-been
Ha-lai-la ha-zeh,
ku-la-nu m'su-been.

שֶׁבְּכָל הַלֵּילוֹת
אָנוּ אוֹכְלִין
בֵּין יוֹשְׁבִין
וּבֵין מְסֻבִּין,
הַלַּיְלָה הַזֶּה
כֻּלָּנוּ מְסֻבִּין.

In Search of the Four Answers

As often happens after the youngest child recites the four questions, the family and guests applaud but do not bother to answer the questions. Since a young child's questions should not go unanswered, we shall present one answer to each, but there are many more answers.

Otto Geismar, 1927

ON ONE HAND, the matza and the maror belong to the menu of the slaves and the oppressed:

1. Why eat plain matza which is hard to digest?
Poor laborers and slaves are fed matza not only because it is cheap but because it is filling and requires a long digestion period. The diet was designed by the oppressor to exploit the people efficiently.

2. Why eat raw, bitter vegetables?
Maror is eaten plain only by the most oppressed workers who are given little time to prepare their meals. With more time they would have made these herbs into a tasty salad.

ON THE OTHER HAND, dipping and reclining typify the manners of the leisure class in Roman times:

3. Why dip twice before eating?
On Seder night we are obligated to dip twice – karpas in salt water and maror in charoset – before the meal begins. Even today, finger foods dipped in tangy sauces are typical hors d'œuvres with cocktails (the first cup of wine) at banquets.

4. Why recline on pillows while drinking wine?
The body language of the free reflects their ease and comfort. Reclining on sofas or pillows, everyone – big and small alike – experiences the freedom of the upper classes. On Seder night these foods and these table manners are props and stage directions in the script acted out by all. *(based on Don Isaac Abrabanel, Zevach Pesach, Spain, 15th C.)*

"Izzy, Did You Ask a Good Question Today?"

Isidor I. Rabi, the Nobel laureate in physics was once asked, "Why did you become a scientist, rather than a doctor or lawyer or businessman, like the other immigrant kids in your neighborhood?"

"My mother made me a scientist without ever intending it. Every other Jewish mother in Brooklyn would ask her child after school: '**Nu? Did you learn anything today?**' But not my mother. She always asked me a different question. '**Izzy**,' she would say, '**Did you ask a good question today**?' That difference – asking good questions – made me become a scientist." *(Donald Sheff, New York Times, Jan. 19, 1988)*

It is an old saying: Ask a Jew a question, and the Jew answers with a question. Every answer given arouses new questions. The progress of knowledge is matched by an increase in the hidden and mysterious.
(Rabbi Leo Baeck, Judaism and Science, Germany, 1949)

A wise person's question is half the answer.
(Shlomo Ibn Gabirol, Spain, 1050)

The Rabbis as Storytellers
Shmuel's Story: "We were slaves"

עֲבָדִים הָיִינוּ

Kadesh
Urchatz
Karpas
Yachatz
Maggid

We Were
Slaves

Storytelling Options

The Haggadah recommends that parents now go beyond the text of the Haggadah and improvise dramatically in retelling the story of the Exodus. The traditional Haggadah does not include a script for the storyteller. For ideas, turn to pages 86-91.

When, in time to come, your children ask you: "What is the meaning of the decrees, laws, and rules that Adonai our God has enjoined upon you?" You shall say to your children: **"We were slaves to Pharaoh in Egypt and Adonai freed us from Egypt with a mighty hand and an outstretched arm.** Adonai produced before our eyes great and awful signs and wonders in Egypt, against Pharaoh and all his household; and God freed us from there, so that God could take us and give us the land that had been promised on oath to our ancestors" *(Deut. 6:20-23).*

"עֲבָדִים הָיִינוּ לְפַרְעֹה בְּמִצְרָיִם. וַיּוֹצִיאֵנוּ יְיָ אֱלֹהֵינוּ מִשָּׁם, בְּיָד חֲזָקָה וּבִזְרוֹעַ נְטוּיָה."

Optional Song:

עֲבָדִים הָיִינוּ, הָיִינוּ
עַתָּה בְּנֵי־חוֹרִין, בְּנֵי־חוֹרִין.

*Avadeem hayeenu, hayeenu,
Ata bnei choreen, bnei choreen*

What if

IF GOD hadn't taken our ancestors out of Egypt, then we would still be enslaved to Pharaoh in Egypt, along with our children, and our children's children.

EVEN IF all of us were wise, all of us discerning, all of us veteran scholars, and all of us knowledgeable in Torah, it would still be a mitzvah for us to retell the story of the Exodus from Egypt.

THE MORE and the longer one expands and embellishes the story, the more commendable.

וְאִלּוּ לֹא הוֹצִיא הַקָּדוֹשׁ בָּרוּךְ הוּא אֶת אֲבוֹתֵינוּ מִמִּצְרַיִם, הֲרֵי אָנוּ וּבָנֵינוּ וּבְנֵי בָנֵינוּ, מְשֻׁעְבָּדִים הָיִינוּ לְפַרְעֹה בְּמִצְרָיִם.

וַאֲפִילוּ כֻּלָּנוּ חֲכָמִים, כֻּלָּנוּ נְבוֹנִים, כֻּלָּנוּ זְקֵנִים, כֻּלָּנוּ יוֹדְעִים אֶת הַתּוֹרָה, מִצְוָה עָלֵינוּ לְסַפֵּר בִּיצִיאַת מִצְרָיִם.

וְכָל הַמַּרְבֶּה לְסַפֵּר בִּיצִיאַת מִצְרָיִם, הֲרֵי זֶה מְשֻׁבָּח.

(Now adults are invited to retell the Exodus story in their own words, or to read aloud one story about Moshe, p. 87-90.)

The Longest Seder: The Five Rabbis of Bnai B'rak

בְּנֵי בְּרַק

A TALE OF Rabbi Eliezer, Rabbi Yehoshua, Rabbi Elazar son of Azarya, Rabbi Akiva and Rabbi Tarfon: they were reclining at the Seder in Bnai B'rak, and they spent the whole night long telling the story of the going out of Egypt, until their pupils came and said to them: "Our masters, it is time to recite the morning Sh'ma!"

מַעֲשֶׂה בְּרַבִּי אֱלִיעֶזֶר, וְרַבִּי יְהוֹשֻׁעַ, וְרַבִּי אֶלְעָזָר בֶּן עֲזַרְיָה, וְרַבִּי עֲקִיבָא, וְרַבִּי טַרְפוֹן, שֶׁהָיוּ מְסֻבִּין בִּבְנֵי בְּרַק, וְהָיוּ מְסַפְּרִים בִּיצִיאַת מִצְרַיִם, כָּל אוֹתוֹ הַלַּיְלָה, עַד שֶׁבָּאוּ תַלְמִידֵיהֶם וְאָמְרוּ לָהֶם: רַבּוֹתֵינוּ, הִגִּיעַ זְמַן קְרִיאַת שְׁמַע, שֶׁל שַׁחֲרִית.

Otto Geismar, 1927

Recalling the Exodus Every Night

RABBI ELAZAR son of Azarya said: "Even though I am like a man of seventy, I had never understood why the going out from Egypt should be mentioned at night-time, until **ben Zoma** explained it to me from the verse, *'That you may remember the day when you came out of Egypt all the days of your life'* (Deuteronomy 16:3).

'The days of your life' means just the days! BUT *'All the days of your life'* means the nights as well!"

However the **Rabbis** explain:

"*'The days of your life'* means this life!

BUT *'All the days of your life'* means the days of the Messiah as well!"

אָמַר רַבִּי אֶלְעָזָר בֶּן עֲזַרְיָה. הֲרֵי אֲנִי כְּבֶן שִׁבְעִים שָׁנָה, וְלֹא זָכִיתִי, שֶׁתֵּאָמֵר יְצִיאַת מִצְרַיִם בַּלֵּילוֹת. עַד שֶׁדְּרָשָׁהּ בֶּן זוֹמָא. שֶׁנֶּאֱמַר: "לְמַעַן תִּזְכֹּר, אֶת יוֹם צֵאתְךָ מֵאֶרֶץ מִצְרַיִם, כֹּל יְמֵי חַיֶּיךָ."
"יְמֵי חַיֶּיךָ" – הַיָּמִים. "כֹּל יְמֵי חַיֶּיךָ" – הַלֵּילוֹת. וַחֲכָמִים אוֹמְרִים: "יְמֵי חַיֶּיךָ" – הָעוֹלָם הַזֶּה. "כֹּל יְמֵי חַיֶּיךָ" – לְהָבִיא לִימוֹת הַמָּשִׁיחַ.

Personal Recollections: "My Most Unusual Seder"

The Seder is as much a family renewal ceremony as a remembrance of ancient Egypt. Sharing family memories with the younger members as well as involving the guests, who may feel homesick, will contribute to the bonding of all participants.

1. Ask the participants, especially the guests, to share a special Seder memory from home or from their most unusual Seder. (See *The Leader's Guide*, pp. 47-54 for great Seders in Jewish history).

2. Ask the participants, especially the oldest ones, to recall their best or their worst moment at the old family Seder. (For example, the Seder when I had stage fright in the middle of the four questions).

The Four Children

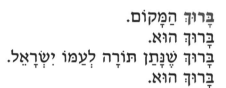

כְּנֶגֶד אַרְבָּעָה בָנִים

1. **The Haggadah** offers us educational advice about intergenerational storytelling. The midrash of the Four Children invites us to distinguish different character types and to suggest different approaches to our offspring. **Consider** the artistic interpretations of the Four Children, and compare and contrast them.

2. **The Rabbis** turn the commandment of "v'heegadta" (you shall **tell**) into a mitzvah of **dialogue** – with give and take on both sides. Successful dialogue means that each side, and especially the side anxious to "pass on the message," be keenly attentive to what the other is saying and feeling – to the particular personality and his or her needs.

Kadesh
Urchatz
Karpas
Yachatz
Maggid

Four
Children

BLESSED be God
Blessed be He
Blessed be the Giver of the Torah to the people Israel
Blessed be He.

THE TORAH alludes to **Four** Children:
One Wise, **One** Wicked, **One** Simple,
One Who Does Not Know How to Ask.

בָּרוּךְ הַמָּקוֹם.
בָּרוּךְ הוּא.
בָּרוּךְ שֶׁנָּתַן תּוֹרָה לְעַמּוֹ יִשְׂרָאֵל.
בָּרוּךְ הוּא.

כְּנֶגֶד אַרְבָּעָה בָנִים דִּבְּרָה תוֹרָה.
אֶחָד חָכָם, וְאֶחָד רָשָׁע, וְאֶחָד תָּם,
וְאֶחָד שֶׁאֵינוֹ יוֹדֵעַ לִשְׁאוֹל.

Istavan Zador, Four Children (Budapest, 1924)

Education Through Dialogue

A Reminder for Parents

Thus far the Haggadah has given guidelines to the parent who is full of earnest enthusiasm to pass on an historical and cultural "message" to the younger generation. If ever there was an event which appeals to the parent's desire to bring their youth-culture-centered children to appreciate the old values of cultural and ethnic pride and identification, the Pesach Seder is it!

Here lies a dangerous pitfall for the parent-educator. The leader of the Seder is likely to concentrate on the text of the Haggadah without sufficiently taking into consideration the audience – the younger generation – and their level of interest. Absorbed with the sales-pitch, the salesperson often forgets the customer!

Prague, 1526

"The Four Parents:" Children Label Their Parents

IN THE DAYS of the patriarchal regime, we allowed ourselves to categorize our children harshly, accepting only one as positive – the wise one.

The simple, the wicked and the one who knows not how to ask questions had to swallow hard and hide their sense of being insulted . . .

Now in our days no child is identified as "the offspring of the parent" and often the parent is identified as "the parent of that child." We have arrived at an era not of partiarchy or matriarchy but the rule of children. In our age it is then miraculous that our dear, delightful children don't divide us up and categorize us. At the best, we would be rated "naive or simple minded parents" or "parents who don't know how to respond to a question." *(Israel Eldad, "The Victory of the Wise Son")*

The Pitfalls of Labelling

I INSTINCTIVELY recoil from static stereotypes that label persons simplistically. Therefore, I choose to interpret the midrash of the four children as a diverse set of strategies for addressing four different facets of each and every child. Each personality combines these facets in different ways. For example, **the wise** and **the rebellious facets** can be combined for evil. Then the cunning mind is used to inflict pain on one's parents. Alternatively, the combination can produce a revolutionary chalutz (pioneer) seeking not just to undermine the traditional order but to create new frameworks of meaning. This requires an intelligence which is not conservative like the traditional "wise child" but which looks beyond the horizon, beyond the existing laws and their pat rationale.

(Yaariv Ben Aharon, Kibbutz author)

Questioning Our Wisdom

The truly wise question the wisdom of others because they question their own wisdom as well, the foolish, because it is different from their own.

Rabbi Leopold Stein, Journey into the Self (Germany, d. 1882)

The Four Children as a Screenplay

חָכָם וְרָשָׁע

1. **A simple reading** of the Haggadah's midrash of the four children can obscure the fact that it provides the script for a dialogue. Let each character in the dialogue be played by a different Seder participant.

2. **The cast** is as follows: - Narrator
- Each of the four children
- Four parents who answer.

3. **The reading** goes as follows:

Kadesh
Urchatz
Karpas
Yachatz
Maggid

Four
Children

Narrator:	**What does the wise child say?**	
Wise Child:	"What are the testimonies, the statutes, and the laws which Adonai our God has commanded you?" *(Deut. 6:20).*	
Narrator:	You must tell some of the laws of Pesach (from the Mishna, for example):	
1st Parent:	"We do not proceed to any *afikoman* (dessert or after dinner celebrations) after eating the Pesach lamb" *(Mishna Pesachim chapter 10).*	

חָכָם מַה הוּא אוֹמֵר?

"מָה הָעֵדֹת וְהַחֻקִּים וְהַמִּשְׁפָּטִים, אֲשֶׁר צִוָּה יְיָ אֱלֹהֵינוּ אֶתְכֶם?" (דברים ו, כ)

וְאַף אַתָּה אֱמָר לוֹ כְּהִלְכוֹת הַפֶּסַח: "אֵין מַפְטִירִין אַחַר הַפֶּסַח אֲפִיקוֹמָן." (משנה, פסחים פרק י')

Narrator:	**What does the wicked child say?**	
Wicked Child:	"Whatever does this service mean to *you?*" *(Exodus 12:26).*	
Narrator:	This child emphasizes "*to you*" and not to himself or herself! Since the child excludes himself or herself from the community and rejects a major principle of faith, you should "set that child's teeth on edge" and say:	
2nd Parent:	"It is because of this, that Adonai did for *me* when *I* went free from Egypt" *(Exodus 13:8).*	
	"*Me*" and not *that one!* Had *that one* been there, he or she would not have been redeemed.	

רָשָׁע מַה הוּא אוֹמֵר?

"מָה הָעֲבֹדָה הַזֹּאת לָכֶם?" (שמות יב, כו) "לָכֶם" וְלֹא "לוֹ!"

וּלְפִי שֶׁהוֹצִיא אֶת עַצְמוֹ מִן הַכְּלָל, כָּפַר בְּעִקָּר. וְאַף אַתָּה הַקְהֵה אֶת שִׁנָּיו, וֶאֱמָר לוֹ: "בַּעֲבוּר זֶה, עָשָׂה יְיָ לִי, בְּצֵאתִי מִמִּצְרַיִם" (שמות יג, ח). "לִי" וְלֹא "לוֹ". אִלּוּ הָיָה שָׁם, לֹא הָיָה נִגְאָל.

Embarassing your Parents

This difficult child is determined to embarrass us, the parents (in the midst of the Seder before all the guests). He implies that the wine and lambchops are only for our culinary pleasure when he says pointedly, "This service is for *you*" (not for God). *(Don Isaac Abrabanel, Spain, 15th C.)*

Otto Geismar, the Wise Child and the Wicked Child, 1927

Siegmund Forst, 1958

Beating the Bounds: Producing Wicked Children

THE PASSOVER CELEBRATION is aimed at the child in all of us, allowing us to open our imaginations, to rediscover the lost elements of wonder, pleasure, and hilarity that are captured in this event. Having children at the Seder can help make this happen.

If we make our children unhappy, they will remember Passover, but not fondly. In the British Isles, there is a custom of taking sons out every year to "beat the bounds." Today they use the stick as the boundary markers, but they used to beat the boys at the site of those markers to ensure that they would remember the limits of ancestral property. Beating our ancient heritage into our children's psyches may make them remember, but it is probably the reason so many people remember ritual and ceremony as intrinsically unpleasant.

(Ira Steingroot, Keeping Passover)

"Who is truly Wise?"

The wise child of the Haggadah is portrayed as a knowledgeable, believing and obedient child. This child formulates long complex questions, distinguishes multiple categories of laws, and accepts the God who commanded "us." But let's beware of this stereotyped, academic brainchild. Is this child truly wise?

● **Don Isaac Abrabanel, "The Smart Alec":** "This 'wise-guy' child is arrogant in his 'wisdom.' He shows off the distinctions he can make between types of mitzvot. *'But you teach him the subtleties down to the last detail in the Mishna.'* Let the 'smart-alec' who appears wise in his own eyes see that there is still much for him to learn.

There is twice as much wisdom in these laws as in the question. Let the wise grow in wisdom and in humility."

● **Israel Eldad, "To Know When to Ask":** "No! The wise child does not derive his title from the pretense to know-it-all. One who thinks he possesses wisdom already, does not ask at all. 'One who does not even know how to ask' has a negative trait, typical of the know-it-all. The truly wise child asks genuine questions, not cynically and mockingly like the rebellious child and not superficially like the simple child. He seeks the essence of things, *'What is the true nature of the laws, testimonies and statutes that God has commanded us?'"*

● **The Chassidic Seer of Lublin:** "In my judgment, it is better to be a wicked person who knows he is wicked, than a righteous one who knows that he is righteous. Worst of all is to be a wicked person who thinks he is righteous."

(Menachem HaCohen, Haggadah of HaAm)

The "Wicked Child" – An Unfair Description?

The "wicked" child expresses a sense of alienation from our Jewish heritage. In this age of liberalism and democracy, of pluralistic tolerance for many cultural expressions, should a person who expresses such a feeling be condemned as "wicked" or "evil"?

● Hold a brief discussion on the topic. Would a different characterization be more appropriate to our contemporary sensibilities - such as "the rebellious one," "the skeptic," "the arrogant – *chutzpadik*?"

Is "setting his teeth on edge" the best strategy to deal with such a person?

● Role-Playing: try to "get inside" the personality of the so called "wicked" children and their parents. Describe the feelings of each one in this tense confrontation described in the Haggadah.

Suggestion: Have the younger participants at the Seder describe the feelings of the parent, and have those who are already parents describe the feelings of the child.

The Four Children Continued

Narrator: **What does the simple child ask?**

Simple Child: "What is this?" *(Exodus 13:14).*

Narrator: And you shall say to that child:

3rd Parent: "By a mighty hand Adonai brought us out of Egypt, out of the house of bondage."

Narrator: **As for the child who does not know how to ask**, you should prompt him, as it is said: "You shall tell your child on that day, saying:"

4th Parent: "It is because of this, that Adonai did for me when I went free from Egypt" *(Exodus 13:8).*

Otto Geismar, 1927

Kadesh
Urchatz
Karpas
Yachatz
Maggid

Four
Children

תָּם וְשֶׁאֵינוֹ יוֹדֵעַ לִשְׁאוֹל

תָּם מַה הוּא אוֹמֵר?

"מַה זֹּאת?" (שמות יג, יד)

"וְאָמַרְתָּ אֵלָיו:

בְּחֹזֶק יָד הוֹצִיאָנוּ יְיָ מִמִּצְרַיִם מִבֵּית עֲבָדִים".

וְשֶׁאֵינוֹ יוֹדֵעַ לִשְׁאוֹל?

אַתְּ פְּתַח לוֹ.

שֶׁנֶּאֱמַר: "וְהִגַּדְתָּ לְבִנְךָ, בַּיּוֹם הַהוּא לֵאמֹר:

'בַּעֲבוּר זֶה עָשָׂה יְיָ לִי, בְּצֵאתִי מִמִּצְרָיִם'." (שמות יג, ח)

The Parent of the Silent Child

The child does not ask because he is afraid of making a mistake. He does not know how to phrase his question and lacks confidence. Therefore, the parent should try to lead him into a conversation, to encourage him, to strengthen him, to strengthen his confidence. (Marc Angel, Sephardic Haggadah, p. 30)

"You shall tell your child" *(Exodus 13:8)*

The Rabbis wondered about: "*You shall tell your child on that day: 'It is because of this, that Adonai did for me when I went free from Egypt.'*"

Could this verse mean that you should begin to tell the story at the beginning of the month (in which the Exodus occurred)?

No, for the verse explicitly states "*on that day*" (of the Exodus). Could that mean that we start when it is still daytime?

No, for the verse explicitly states: "*because of this.*" "**This**" refers to matza and marror laid before you (only on Seder night). *(Mekhilta)*

"**This**" implies that the parents must point at the matza and marror, using them as visual aids to tell the story. *(Rabbi Simcha of Vitri)*

וְהִגַּדְתָּ לְבִנְךָ

"וְהִגַּדְתָּ לְבִנְךָ". יָכוֹל מֵרֹאשׁ חֹדֶשׁ?

תַּלְמוּד לוֹמַר: "בַּיּוֹם הַהוּא" (שמות י"ג ח).

אִי בַּיּוֹם הַהוּא, יָכוֹל מִבְּעוֹד יוֹם?

תַּלְמוּד לוֹמַר: "בַּעֲבוּר זֶה."

"בַּעֲבוּר זֶה", לֹא אָמַרְתִּי, אֶלָּא בְּשָׁעָה שֶׁיֵּשׁ

מַצָּה וּמָרוֹר מֻנָּחִים לְפָנֶיךָ.

The Contemporary "Four Children"

Which famous person today would be the best representative of the "wise child," of the "wicked child," and so on? Suggest candidates and discuss their suitability. Or suggest animals to symbolize the Four Children. (See p. 29.)

A Child's Perspective

Ask the younger children to describe the behavior of "a bad child" at the Seder.
- What might be causing such behavior?
- Do they approve of the parent's response in the Haggadah?
- How would they handle the situation?
- Why do they think the "silent child" asks no questions?
- How might that child be coaxed into greater involvement?

Beyond Labels

I DO NOT VIEW labels as static pigeon-holes. I believe in the power of the educational act to release locked up potentials. For example, **one who does not know how to ask** may be silenced by the rules of society. The silence may hide an exceptional, sensitive child whose questions are choked. A parent can "open the child up," remove the obstructions, enable personal growth and break stereotypes *(Yaariv Ben Aharon, Kibbutz author)*.

The Immigrant Family   *Chicago Haggadah, 1879*

Bridging the Generation Gap

The inter-generational dialogues in the Torah explicitly refer to parents who participated in the Exodus addressing their children who have grown up in freedom in the Land of Israel. The parents have undergone an experience of slavery and redemption which is totally foreign to the reality of their offspring.

Discussion #1: What are the generation gaps among us, the participants of tonight's Seder? Go around the table and have people relate a formative experience which might be difficult for their parents or children to comprehend.

Discussion #2: In the illustration above, who do the characters represent? How do their clothing and body language express the generation gap? Who is the dominant figure at the table?

23

The Art of the Four Children

1. **Compare and contrast** the artists' interpretations of each of the Four Children (p. 18-33).

2. **Which portrayal** is most surprising? most disturbing? most appropriate?

3. **What conceptions** of Jewish values and society are implicit in the various depictions? (See the unabridged version of A Different Night, p. 174-176, for a commentary on each illustration.)

The Ideal Jewish Girl?
Tanya Zion, Israel, 1996

Kadesh
Urchatz
Karpas
Yachatz
Maggid

Four
Children
in Art

CINDERELLA? DEBORA THE PROPHETESS? MADONNA? GOLDA MEIR? RABBI?

LAWYER? DOCTOR? MOTHER? WIFE? I.D.F. PILOT? SPORTSWOMAN? ACTRESS?

THE "BAD" CHILD   חרשע

THE "WISE" CHILD   חכמה

THE "GOOD GIRL" SIMPLE CHILD   תמימה

THE ONE WHO DOES NOT ASK...   שאינה יודעת לשאול

POLICE

Barbie

Eastern European Types

Arthur Szyk,
Poland, 1939

בָּרוּךְ הַמָּקוֹם
הוּא בָּרוּךְ

כְּנֶגֶד אַרְבָּעָה
וְאֶחָד חָכָם,
רָשָׁע,

לְכֶם וְלֹא לוֹ. וּלְפִי שֶׁהוֹצִיא
אֶת עַצְמוֹ מִן הַכְּלָל כָּפַר בְּעִקָּר
אַף אַתָּה הַקְהֵה אֶת שִׁנָּיו וְאֵל
וֶאֱמוֹר לוֹ : בַּעֲבוּר זֶה, עָשָׂה יְיָ
לִי בְּצֵאתִי מִמִּצְרַיִם. לִי וְלֹא לוֹ.
אִלּוּ הָיָה שָׁם לֹא הָיָה נִגְאָל.

וְאַף אַתָּה אֱמוֹר לוֹ כְּהִלְכוֹת
הַפֶּסַח אֵין מַפְטִירִין אַחַר ה
הַפֶּסַח אֲפִיקוֹמָן.

The Blessing of Diversity

The artist and calligrapher David Moss explains his depiction of the Four Children:

EVERY CHILD is unique and the Torah embraces them all. The iconography that I've chosen here is based on playing cards. As in a game of chance, we have no control over the children dealt us. It is our task as parents, as educators, to play our hand based on the attributes of the children we are given. It is the child, not the parent, who must direct the process. This, I believe, is the intent of the midrash of the four children.

Each child's question appears on his card, and the Haggadah's answer appears below the card. The gold object in each picture denotes the suit of the card. The staves, swords, cups and coins used in Southern Europe developed parallel to the more familiar hearts, diamonds, clubs and spades of Northern Europe. The figures are likewise taken from archaic systems of playing cards which included king, knight, page, and joker or fool.

The king image here represents the wise child wearing the crown of Torah. The knight represents the wicked child. In almost all old haggadot the wicked child is shown as a soldier, sometimes mounted, sometimes on foot. The page is the simple child, and the joker or fool is the child who is not even capable of asking.

Every Child is a Blessing

I got the idea of representing the children as cards, by the way, from the tradition dating from the Middle Ages of depicting the simple child, or the child who doesn't know how to ask, as a jester or fool. I drew a book in each picture and positioned it to reflect each child's attitude to the tradition.

The text of the Haggadah introduces the four children with a short passage in which the word *baruch* (blessed) appears four times. I have designed these two pages to correlate each of these four "blessings" with one of the four children: every child is a blessing.

Diversity, how we deal with it, and how we can discover the blessing within it, is perhaps the theme of the midrash of the Four Children.

(David Moss, 20th C. artist, U.S.A. and Israel)

The Blessing of Diversity.
David Moss,
The Moss Haggadah © 1996

27

Four Attitudes to the Zionist Dream

Tzvi Livni, Israel, 1955 © Yavneh Publishers

Four Personalities   *Paul Freeman, U.S.A., 1960*   *Clashing Cultures*   *Sigmund Forst, Europe and U.S.A., 1959*

29

73/125

Shraga Weil '67

Four Children, Four Musicians

Shraga Weil, (CL 1963 Cat. S-3) © Safrai Gallery

30

Four Aspects in Each of Us   *Dan Reisinger, © 1982, Rabbinical Assembly of America*

בם מה הוא אומר
מה זאת?

ת

חכם מה הוא אומר
מה העדות והחקים
והמשפטים אשר צוה יי
אלהינו אתכם?

שאינו יודע לשאל
את פתח לו?

רשע מה הוא אומר
מה העבדה הזאת
לכם?

ר

שע

The Four Children as Four Books   *David Wander, The Haggadah in Memory of the Holocaust © 1988*

Clay Children   *Rony Oren, Animated Haggadah, © 1985 Jonathan Lubell, Scopus Films*

שְׁאֵינוֹ
יוֹדֵעַ לִשְׁאוֹל · תָּם · רָשָׁע · חָכָם

Nota Koslowsky, U.S.A, 1944

Lola, U.S.A, 1920

Jakob Steinhardt, Germany, 1923

Dick Codor © 1981

33

Rav's Pesach Story
From Serving Idols to Spiritual Liberation

מִתְּחִלָּה עוֹבְדֵי
עֲבוֹדָה זָרָה

1. *The Haggadah offers two versions of the Exodus story. The Talmudic Rabbi, **Shmuel**, emphasized political enslavement ("We were slaves in Egypt"). Now we turn to his colleague, Rav, to hear about spiritual servitude.*

2. ***Rav's version** is drawn from Joshua's farewell speech to the nation of Israel. Joshua feared that the new generation in Israel might assimilate to the local pagan cultures. So he told them the story of Abraham's liberation from idolatry.*

Kadesh
Urchatz
Karpas
Yachatz
Maggid

Spiritual Slavery and Keeping the Promise

IN THE BEGINNING our ancestors were idol worshippers But now God has brought us near to serve Adonai.

The leader:

JOSHUA said to all the people: "Thus said Adonai the God of Israel: Long ago your ancestors including Terach, father of Abraham and Nachor, lived beyond the Euphrates and worshipped other gods. But I took your father Abraham from beyond the Euphrates and led him through the whole land of Canaan and multiplied his offspring. I gave him Isaac, and to Isaac I gave Jacob and Esau . . . Then Jacob and his children went down to Egypt."

"Then I sent Moses and Aaron, and brought plagues on Egypt after which I freed you – I freed your ancestors – from Egypt. Now, therefore, serve Adonai with undivided loyalty. . . . Or, if you are loath to serve Adonai, choose this day other gods to serve. But I and my family will serve Adonai."

All:

IN REPLY, the people declared, "Far be it from us to forsake Adonai and serve other gods! For it was Adonai our God who brought us and our ancestors up from the land of Egypt, the house of bondage, and who performed those wondrous signs before our very eyes . . . Now we too will serve Adonai, for Adonai is our God" *(Joshua 24: 1-18).*

מִתְּחִלָּה עוֹבְדֵי עֲבוֹדָה זָרָה הָיוּ אֲבוֹתֵינוּ.
וְעַכְשָׁו קֵרְבָנוּ הַמָּקוֹם לַעֲבוֹדָתוֹ. שֶׁנֶּאֱמַר (יהושע כ"ד):

"וַיֹּאמֶר יְהוֹשֻׁעַ אֶל כָּל הָעָם:
'כֹּה אָמַר יְיָ אֱלֹהֵי יִשְׂרָאֵל,
בְּעֵבֶר הַנָּהָר יָשְׁבוּ אֲבוֹתֵיכֶם מֵעוֹלָם, תֶּרַח אֲבִי
אַבְרָהָם וַאֲבִי נָחוֹר, וַיַּעַבְדוּ אֱלֹהִים אֲחֵרִים.
וָאֶקַּח אֶת אֲבִיכֶם אֶת אַבְרָהָם מֵעֵבֶר הַנָּהָר,
וָאוֹלֵךְ אוֹתוֹ בְּכָל אֶרֶץ כְּנָעַן.
וָאַרְבֶּה אֶת זַרְעוֹ, וָאֶתֵּן לוֹ אֶת יִצְחָק.
וָאֶתֵּן לְיִצְחָק אֶת יַעֲקֹב וְאֶת עֵשָׂו.
וָאֶתֵּן לְעֵשָׂו אֶת הַר שֵׂעִיר, לָרֶשֶׁת אוֹתוֹ.
וְיַעֲקֹב וּבָנָיו יָרְדוּ מִצְרָיִם.'"

Jews-by-Choice

Abraham and Sarah were converts who as mature adults made daring spiritual choices. Today many of us are really Jews-by-choice (whether as converts or as born Jews). For we continuously reflect on our life choices and make decisions about how Jewishly to live. Ask several people to share their personal journey as Jews.

Keeping the Promise

בָּרוּךְ שׁוֹמֵר הַבְטָחָתוֹ

After recalling Abraham's spiritual journey to God (p. 34) and his **ascent** to Eretz Yisrael, the Haggadah will recount the **descent** of his great grandchildren to Egyptian slavery ("The Wandering Aramean," p. 36). But first the Haggadah reassures us, as God did to Abraham, that there is a Divine pledge to Jewish continuity whatever the ups and downs of history.

The leader:

BLESSED is the One who keeps the Promise to Israel. The Holy One Blessed be He calculated the end of our exile and acted just as promised to Abraham our Father at the Covenant between the Pieces *(Genesis 15: 7-17)*:

"And God said to Abram: You must know that your seed will be strangers in a land not theirs; the people (of that land) will put them in servitude and afflict them for four hundred years. But as for the nation to which they are in servitude – I will bring judgment on them, and after that (your seed) will go out with great wealth" *(Genesis 15: 13-14)*.

בָּרוּךְ שׁוֹמֵר הַבְטָחָתוֹ לְיִשְׂרָאֵל, בָּרוּךְ הוּא. שֶׁהַקָּדוֹשׁ בָּרוּךְ הוּא חִשַּׁב אֶת הַקֵּץ, לַעֲשׂוֹת כְּמָה שֶׁאָמַר לְאַבְרָהָם אָבִינוּ בִּבְרִית בֵּין הַבְּתָרִים, שֶׁנֶּאֱמַר (בראשית טו, יג):

"וַיֹּאמֶר לְאַבְרָם יָדֹעַ תֵּדַע, כִּי גֵר יִהְיֶה זַרְעֲךָ, בְּאֶרֶץ לֹא לָהֶם, וַעֲבָדוּם וְעִנּוּ אֹתָם אַרְבַּע מֵאוֹת שָׁנָה. וְגַם אֶת הַגּוֹי אֲשֶׁר יַעֲבֹדוּ דָן אָנֹכִי. וְאַחֲרֵי כֵן יֵצְאוּ, בִּרְכֻשׁ גָּדוֹל."

E. M. Lilien

Standing Up For Us

וְהִיא שֶׁעָמְדָה

1. *Cover the matza, raise your cup and sing together, acknowledging God's commitment to our survival.*

2. *Afterwards, set the cup down and uncover the matza for the continuation of Maggid.*

THIS PROMISE has stood for our parents and for us in good stead.
For not just one enemy has stood against us to wipe us out.
But in every generation there have been those who have stood against us to wipe us out,
Yet the Holy One, Blessed be He,
keeps on saving us from their hands.

V'hee she-am-da,
la-a-vo-tei-nu v'la-nu,
she-lo eh-chad beel-vad,
amad alei-nu l'cha-lo-tei-nu
eh-la she-b'chol dor va-dor
om-deem a-lei-nu l'cha-lo-tei-nu,
v'ha-ka-dosh ba-ruch hu
ma-tzee-lei-nu mee-ya-dam.

וְהִיא שֶׁעָמְדָה לַאֲבוֹתֵינוּ וְלָנוּ. שֶׁלֹּא אֶחָד בִּלְבָד, עָמַד עָלֵינוּ לְכַלּוֹתֵנוּ. אֶלָּא שֶׁבְּכָל דּוֹר וָדוֹר, עוֹמְדִים עָלֵינוּ לְכַלּוֹתֵנוּ, וְהַקָּדוֹשׁ בָּרוּךְ הוּא מַצִּילֵנוּ מִיָּדָם.

"Arami Oved Avi"
The Wandering Jew

אֲרַמִּי אֹבֵד אָבִי

On Seder night we recall that we were once "Wandering Jews," characters in a story of rags to riches, slavery to freedom (Deuteronomy 26).

We are urged to discuss these themes in a mini-symposium at the table, as the five rabbis at Bnai Brak once did, even for a whole night long.

Kadesh
Urchatz
Karpas
Yachatz
Maggid

Wandering Jew

The Torah: A Tale of Persecution and Homecoming

Narrator:
When you enter the land that Adonai your God is giving you as an inheritance, and you possess it and settle on it, then you shall take some of every first fruit of the soil. Put it in a basket and go to the place where Adonai your God will choose to establish His Name. You will go before the *cohen* (priest) in charge at that time and say to him:

All:
Today I will tell Adonai our God how I have come to the land Adonai swore to our ancestors to give to us . . .

"MY ANCESTOR was a wandering Aramean. He descended to Egypt and resided there in small numbers. He became a nation – great, powerful and numerous. The Egyptians treated us badly. They persecuted us and put us under hard labor. We cried out to Adonai, the God of our ancestors. God heard our voice. God saw our persecution, our toil and our oppression. God took us out of Egypt with a strong hand and an outstretched arm, with awesome power, signs and wonders. God brought us to this place and gave us this land, a land of milk and honey. Now I have brought the first fruits of this soil, which you, God, gave me" *(Deut. 26:1-10).*

Prague, 1526

"אֲרַמִּי אֹבֵד אָבִי, וַיֵּרֶד מִצְרַיְמָה, וַיָּגָר שָׁם
בִּמְתֵי מְעָט. וַיְהִי שָׁם לְגוֹי גָּדוֹל, עָצוּם וָרָב.
וַיָּרֵעוּ אֹתָנוּ הַמִּצְרִים וַיְעַנּוּנוּ.
וַיִּתְּנוּ עָלֵינוּ עֲבֹדָה קָשָׁה.
וַנִּצְעַק אֶל יְיָ אֱלֹהֵי אֲבֹתֵינוּ,
וַיִּשְׁמַע יְיָ אֶת קֹלֵנוּ, וַיַּרְא אֶת עָנְיֵנוּ,
וְאֶת עֲמָלֵנוּ, וְאֶת לַחֲצֵנוּ.
וַיּוֹצִאֵנוּ יְיָ מִמִּצְרַיִם, בְּיָד חֲזָקָה, וּבִזְרֹעַ
נְטוּיָה, וּבְמֹרָא גָּדוֹל וּבְאֹתוֹת וּבְמֹפְתִים,
וַיְבִאֵנוּ אֶל הַמָּקוֹם הַזֶּה וַיִּתֶּן־לָנוּ אֶת הָאָרֶץ
הַזֹּאת אֶרֶץ זָבַת חָלָב וּדְבָשׁ."

36

The Classic Rabbinic Midrash on the Exodus
"The Wandering Aramean"

צֵא וּלְמַד

צֵא וּלְמַד, מַה בִּקֵּשׁ לָבָן הָאֲרַמִּי
לַעֲשׂוֹת לְיַעֲקֹב אָבִינוּ?
שֶׁפַּרְעֹה לֹא גָזַר אֶלָּא עַל הַזְּכָרִים, וְלָבָן בִּקֵּשׁ לַעֲקֹר
אֶת הַכֹּל, שֶׁנֶּאֱמַר (דברים כז, ה):
"אֲרַמִּי אֹבֵד אָבִי."

Read and study:

GO AND LEARN what (awful) plans Lavan the
Aramean had for Jacob our Father:

(When Jacob migrated to Aram, he intended to stay with his
uncle Lavan for only a few months. However, he fell in love with
his cousin Rachel and was entrapped by his wily uncle Lavan the
Aramean whose epithet also means "the cheat" – *ramai.* Jacob
became his indentured servant and escaped with his wives and
children only after 20 years of hard labor. Even then Lavan and
his armed men pursued Jacob intending to do bodily harm, perhaps even to kill him but at least to enslave him again. Had God
not appeared miraculously in a night vision to stay Lavan's
hand, there would have been no people of Israel).

THUS WHILE Pharaoh intended to kill only the boys,
Lavan sought to uproot the whole of Jacob's family,
the children of Israel.

THIS IS the hidden meaning of the verse,
"the wandering Aramean" – the Aramean sought to
exterminate my father – that is, Jacob.

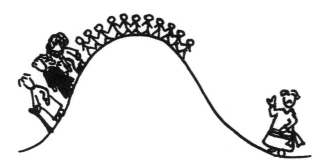

Assimilation and Identity

"ISRAEL (JACOB) DESCENDED TO EGYPT, RESIDED THERE IN SMALL NUMBERS, AND BECAME THERE A NATION – GREAT, POWERFUL AND NUMEROUS" *(Deut. 26:5)*.

"ARAMI אֹבֵד אָבִי, וַיֵּרֶד מִצְרַיְמָה, וַיָּגָר שָׁם בִּמְתֵי מְעָט. וַיְהִי שָׁם לְגוֹי גָּדוֹל, עָצוּם וָרָב."

"ISRAEL DESCENDED" compelled by the divine word, to fulfill the prophecy of God to Abraham that *"your descendants will be strangers in a land not their own, where they will be enslaved and persecuted . . . ."* *(Gen. 14:13)*.

"וַיֵּרֶד מִצְרַיְמָה." אָנוּס עַל פִּי הַדִּבּוּר.

Kadesh
Urchatz
Karpas
Yachatz
Maggid

Symposium:
Assimilation,
Antisemitism

"ISRAEL RESIDED THERE" *(Deut. 26:5)* temporarily. Jacob our Father never intended to settle permanently in Egypt. Jacob's family made that clear from the onset. *"They said to the Pharaoh (who reigned in the days of Joseph): we have come (merely) to **reside** in this land, for there is no pasture for your servants' sheep. For the famine in the land of Canaan is very heavy. Therefore, please permit your servants to stay in the land of Goshen (within Egypt where grazing is good)"* *(Gen. 47:4)*.

"וַיָּגָר שָׁם." מְלַמֵּד שֶׁלֹּא יָרַד יַעֲקֹב אָבִינוּ לְהִשְׁתַּקֵּעַ בְּמִצְרַיִם, אֶלָּא לָגוּר שָׁם, שֶׁנֶּאֱמַר (בראשית מ"ז, ד): "וַיֹּאמְרוּ אֶל פַּרְעֹה: לָגוּר בָּאָרֶץ בָּאנוּ, כִּי אֵין מִרְעֶה לַצֹּאן אֲשֶׁר לַעֲבָדֶיךָ, כִּי כָבֵד הָרָעָב בְּאֶרֶץ כְּנָעַן. וְעַתָּה, יֵשְׁבוּ נָא עֲבָדֶיךָ בְּאֶרֶץ גֹּשֶׁן."

"IN SMALL NUMBERS" *(Deut. 26:5)* Jacob arrived in Egypt. Moshe reminds us that: *"with only seventy persons, your ancestors descended to Egypt. Yet now Adonai your God has made you as numerous as the stars of the sky"* *(Deut.10:22)*.

"בִּמְתֵי מְעָט." כְּמָה שֶׁנֶּאֱמַר (דברים י, כב): "בְּשִׁבְעִים נֶפֶשׁ, יָרְדוּ אֲבֹתֶיךָ מִצְרָיְמָה. וְעַתָּה, שָׂמְךָ יְיָ אֱלֹהֶיךָ, כְּכוֹכְבֵי הַשָּׁמַיִם לָרֹב."

"THERE ISRAEL BECAME A NATION" *(Deut.26:5)* – recognizable, distinctive, standing out from the others.

"וַיְהִי שָׁם לְגוֹי." מְלַמֵּד שֶׁהָיוּ יִשְׂרָאֵל מְצֻיָּנִים שָׁם.

Antisemitism and Prejudice

"A NATION – GREAT AND POWERFUL" *(Deut 26:5)* emerged at an incredible pace. *"The children of Israel were fruitful and swarmed, they multiplied and became very, very powerful. The whole land was filled with them"* *(Exodus 1:7)*.

"A NUMEROUS NATION" *(Deut 26:5)* also means "full-grown" *(rav)*. The prophet captures God's nurturing of Israel in Egypt with graphic imagery. *"I let you grow like the plants of the field. You continued to grow up until you attained womanhood, until your breasts became firm, and your hair flourished. Yet you were still naked (spiritually)"* *(Ezekiel 16:7)*.

"THE EGYPTIANS TREATED US BADLY, THEY PERSECUTED US AND IMPOSED HARD LABOR ON US" *(Deut 26:6)*.

"THE EGYPTIANS TREATED US BADLY" *(Deut 26:6)*, means they "bad-mouthed" our loyalty. Pharaoh set the ominous tone in speaking to his people: *"Let us outsmart them so that they may not increase. Otherwise, in the event of war, they will join our enemies, fight against us and expel us from the land"* *(Exodus 1:10)*.

Prejudice and I

Recount a story in which you were involved in unjust discrimination whether as a victim, a witness or a perpetrator. How do these examples compare to Egyptian persecution of strangers?

"גָּדוֹל עָצוּם." כְּמָה שֶׁנֶּאֱמַר (שמות א, ז): "וּבְנֵי יִשְׂרָאֵל, פָּרוּ וַיִּשְׁרְצוּ, וַיִּרְבּוּ וַיַּעַצְמוּ, בִּמְאֹד מְאֹד, וַתִּמָּלֵא הָאָרֶץ אֹתָם."

"וָרָב." כְּמָה שֶׁנֶּאֱמַר (יחזקאל טז, ז): "רְבָבָה כְּצֶמַח הַשָּׂדֶה נְתַתִּיךְ, וַתִּרְבִּי, וַתִּגְדְּלִי, וַתָּבֹאִי בַּעֲדִי עֲדָיִים. שָׁדַיִם נָכֹנוּ, וּשְׂעָרֵךְ צִמֵּחַ, וְאַתְּ עֵרֹם וְעֶרְיָה."

"וַיָּרֵעוּ אֹתָנוּ הַמִּצְרִים וַיְעַנּוּנוּ. וַיִּתְּנוּ עָלֵינוּ עֲבֹדָה קָשָׁה."

"וַיָּרֵעוּ אֹתָנוּ הַמִּצְרִים." כְּמָה שֶׁנֶּאֱמַר (שמות א, י): "הָבָה נִתְחַכְּמָה לוֹ, פֶּן יִרְבֶּה, וְהָיָה כִּי תִקְרֶאנָה מִלְחָמָה, וְנוֹסַף גַּם הוּא עַל שֹׂנְאֵינוּ, וְנִלְחַם בָּנוּ וְעָלָה מִן הָאָרֶץ."

Ancient Egyptian Oppression

"THEY PERSECUTED US" (Deut. 26:6). *"They put task masters over Israel to conscript their labor in order to persecute them with their burdens. They built for Pharaoh the garrison cities of Pitom* (House of the god Atum) *and Ra-meses* (Domain of the Son of the Sun god)" (Exodus 1:11).

"וַיְעַנּוּנוּ." כְּמָה שֶׁנֶּאֱמַר (שמות א, יא): "וַיָּשִׂימוּ עָלָיו שָׂרֵי מִסִּים, לְמַעַן עַנֹּתוֹ בְּסִבְלֹתָם. וַיִּבֶן עָרֵי מִסְכְּנוֹת לְפַרְעֹה, אֶת פִּתֹם וְאֶת רַעַמְסֵס."

"THEY IMPOSED HARD LABOR ON US" (Deut. 26:6). *"The Egyptians worked the children of Israel harshly (be-farech)"* (Exodus 1:13), degrading us with back-breaking and spirit-crushing labor.

"וַיִּתְּנוּ עָלֵינוּ עֲבֹדָה קָשָׁה." כְּמָה שֶׁנֶּאֱמַר (שמות א, יג): "וַיַּעֲבִדוּ מִצְרַיִם אֶת בְּנֵי יִשְׂרָאֵל בְּפָרֶךְ."

Kadesh
Urchatz
Karpas
Yachatz
Maggid

Symposium: Oppression, Resistance

Midrash: Filling in the Gaps

WHILE THE BIBLE is short on concrete details, the Rabbinic midrash imaginatively reconstructs the daily pain and indignity of slavery from the hints in the text.

1. Why does the Torah use the rare term **"be-farech"** to describe the Egyptian harsh labor?

Rabbi Elazar explained: Don't read *"be-farech"* – "with harshness" but *"be-fe-rach"* – "with soft speech," with a silvery tongue. Pharoah had already declared that the Egyptians must "outsmart" Israel. So he gathered all the children of Israel and gave them this "pitch:" "Please do me a favor today and give me a hand." Pharaoh took up a rake and a basket and began to make mud bricks. Everyone who saw him did likewise. Israel worked with him enthusiastically all day. When it grew dark, Pharoah appointed task masters over them to count up their bricks. "That," he announced, "will be your daily quota!" (Tanhuma Buber, BeHaalotcha).

2. What does the Torah mean when it says, "Moshe went out to his kinsfolk and saw their burdens" (Ex. 2:11)?

Moshe saw a big burden on an old person and a small one on a young healthy person, a woman's task assigned to a man and a man's task assigned to a woman. He began to cry and say, "Oy! I feel so bad for them. I would give my life for them." So he would leave his royal retinue and go join his brothers and sisters. While pretending to be executing Pharoah's orders, he rearranged the burdens, helping each and every slave.

Egyptian slaves making mud bricks mixed with straw and water, dried in wooden frames. Tomb of Rekhmire, 18th Century. B.C.E.

Resignation to Resistance

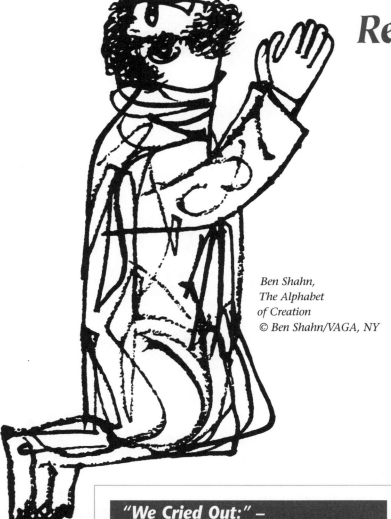

Ben Shahn,
*The Alphabet
of Creation*
© Ben Shahn/VAGA, NY

"וַנִּצְעַק אֶל יְיָ אֱלֹהֵי אֲבֹתֵינוּ, וַיִּשְׁמַע יְיָ אֶת קֹלֵנוּ,
וַיַּרְא אֶת עָנְיֵנוּ, וְאֶת עֲמָלֵנוּ, וְאֶת לַחֲצֵנוּ."

"וַנִּצְעַק אֶל יְיָ אֱלֹהֵי אֲבֹתֵינוּ." כְּמָה שֶׁנֶּאֱמַר (שמות ב, כג):
"וַיְהִי בַיָּמִים הָרַבִּים הָהֵם, וַיָּמָת מֶלֶךְ מִצְרַיִם,
וַיֵּאָנְחוּ בְנֵי יִשְׂרָאֵל מִן הָעֲבֹדָה וַיִּזְעָקוּ.
וַתַּעַל שַׁוְעָתָם אֶל הָאֱלֹהִים מִן הָעֲבֹדָה."

"וַיִּשְׁמַע יְיָ אֶת קֹלֵנוּ." כְּמָה שֶׁנֶּאֱמַר (שמות ב, כד):
"וַיִּשְׁמַע אֱלֹהִים אֶת נַאֲקָתָם, וַיִּזְכֹּר אֱלֹהִים אֶת בְּרִיתוֹ,
אֶת אַבְרָהָם, אֶת יִצְחָק, וְאֶת יַעֲקֹב."

**"WE CRIED OUT TO ADONAI, THE GOD OF OUR
FATHERS, GOD HEARD OUR VOICE, HE SAW OUR
PERSECUTION, OUR TOIL, AND OUR OPPRESSION"**
(Deut. 26:7).

"WE CRIED OUT TO ADONAI" *(Deut. 26:7).* This was the
turning point. *"After many, many days, the king of
Egypt died. The children of Israel groaned from under the
labor and cried out in protest. Their cry for help rose up to
God from their labor"* *(Ex. 2:23).*

"GOD HEARD OUR VOICE" *(Deut. 26:7).*
Just as it says in Exodus : *"God HEARD their moans
and God remembered the Divine covenant with Abraham
and Isaac and Jacob"* *(Exodus 2:24).*

"We Cried Out:" –
The Power of a Groan

THE HASSIDIC Rebbe of Gur says:
The sigh, the groan and the crying out of the
children of Israel from the slavery was the beginning of redemption. As long as they did not cry
out against their exile they were neither worthy
nor ready for redemption *(Menachem HaCohen).*

Sexuality and Liberation

"GOD SAW OUR PERSE-CUTION" *(Deut 26:7)*. The root *"oni"* (persecution) is similar to *"ona"* (marital intimacy), thus hinting at Pharaoh's policy of enforced abstention from *"ona"* (sexual intercourse). Perhaps that is delicately intimated when it says *(Ex. 2:25)* that: *"God saw the children of Israel, and God **knew**"* (their marital suffering, for knowledge has sexual overtones as in *"Adam **knew** his wife Eve"* [Gen. 4:1]).

Shraga Weil,
Song of Songs
© 1968

Kadesh
Urchatz
Karpas
Yachatz
Maggid

Symposium:
Sexual
Liberation

Ten
Plagues

"OUR TOIL" *(Deut. 26:7)* refers to the sons – the lost fruits of our "labor" who were drowned in Egypt. Pharaoh proclaimed: *"Every son who is born shall be cast into the Nile, while every daughter shall live"* *(Ex. 1:22)*.

"OUR OPPRESSION" *(Deut. 26:7)* refers to *"the pressure which the Egyptians applied to them"* *(Ex. 3:9)*.

Women's Resistance

THE EGYPTIANS' expressed purpose in enslaving Israel was to drastically cut their birth rate. The hard labor in the fields exhausted the slaves physically and spiritually. According to a Rabbinic midrash, it was the women who resisted the intent of Pharaoh's decree. They used their sexuality to arouse their husbands, and so re-ignite the fundamental will to life:

> When Israel performed hard labor in Egypt, Pharaoh decreed that the men must not sleep in their homes, so that they would not engage in sexual relations. R. Shimon bar Halafta said: What did the daughters of Israel do? They went down to draw water from the Nile and God would bring little fish into their jars. They cooked some of the fish and sold the rest, buying wine with the proceeds. Then they went out to the fields and fed their husbands. After eating and drinking, the women would take out bronze mirrors and look at them with their husbands. The wife would say "I'm prettier than you," and the husband would reply, "I'm more beautiful than you." Thus they would arouse themselves to desire and they would then "be fruitful and multiply."

"וַיַּרְא אֶת עָנְיֵנוּ." זוֹ פְּרִישׁוּת דֶּרֶךְ אֶרֶץ. כְּמָה שֶׁנֶּאֱמַר
(שמות ב, כה): "וַיַּרְא אֱלֹהִים אֶת בְּנֵי יִשְׂרָאֵל.
וַיֵּדַע אֱלֹהִים."

"וְאֶת עֲמָלֵנוּ." אֵלּוּ הַבָּנִים. כְּמָה שֶׁנֶּאֱמַר (שמות א, כב):
"כָּל הַבֵּן הַיִּלּוֹד הַיְאֹרָה תַּשְׁלִיכֻהוּ, וְכָל הַבַּת תְּחַיּוּן."

"וְאֶת לַחֲצֵנוּ." זֶה הַדְּחַק. כְּמָה שֶׁנֶּאֱמַר (שמות ג, ט):
"וְגַם רָאִיתִי אֶת הַלַּחַץ, אֲשֶׁר מִצְרַיִם לֹחֲצִים אֹתָם."

The Ten Plagues
God's Strong Hand, His Outstretched Arm, and His Little Finger

עֶשֶׂר מַכּוֹת

1. **The main ceremony** of removing ten drops of wine for the Ten Plagues is on page 46. (Some may wish to skip directly to that climax of the lengthy Rabbinic discussion of the Ten Plagues).

2. **The Rabbis** debated about the Ten Plagues:

On the one hand, they were a necessary instrument of liberation and a just punishment for Egyptian cruelty. Yet, on the other, they involved the suffering of fellow human beings. "We celebrate the Exodus from Egypt, not the downfall of the Egyptians." (Rabbi Simcha Cohen)

"GOD TOOK US OUT OF EGYPT WITH A STRONG HAND, AND AN OUTSTRETCHED ARM, WITH AWESOME POWER, SIGNS AND WONDERS" (Deut. 26:8).

"וַיּוֹצִאֵנוּ יְיָ מִמִּצְרַיִם, בְּיָד חֲזָקָה, וּבִזְרֹעַ נְטוּיָה, וּבְמֹרָא גָּדוֹל וּבְאֹתוֹת וּבְמֹפְתִים."

"GOD TOOK US OUT" (Deut. 26:8) –
Not by the hands of an angel, . . .
Not by the hands of a messenger,
But the Holy One Blessed Be He Himself in His own Glory.
Just as it says, *"I will pass through the land of Egypt, and I will strike down every first born in Egypt, both human and beast, I will execute judgment on all the gods of Egypt, I am God"* (Ex. 12:12).

"וַיּוֹצִאֵנוּ יְיָ מִמִּצְרַיִם." לֹא עַל יְדֵי מַלְאָךְ, וְלֹא עַל יְדֵי שָׂרָף, וְלֹא עַל יְדֵי שָׁלִיחַ, אֶלָּא הַקָּדוֹשׁ בָּרוּךְ הוּא בִּכְבוֹדוֹ וּבְעַצְמוֹ. שֶׁנֶּאֱמַר (שמות יב, יב):
"וְעָבַרְתִּי בְאֶרֶץ מִצְרַיִם בַּלַּיְלָה הַזֶּה, וְהִכֵּיתִי כָל בְּכוֹר בְּאֶרֶץ מִצְרַיִם, מֵאָדָם וְעַד בְּהֵמָה, וּבְכָל אֱלֹהֵי מִצְרַיִם אֶעֱשֶׂה שְׁפָטִים, אֲנִי יְיָ."

"וְעָבַרְתִּי בְאֶרֶץ מִצְרַיִם בַּלַּיְלָה הַזֶּה" – אֲנִי וְלֹא מַלְאָךְ. "וְהִכֵּיתִי כָל בְּכוֹר בְּאֶרֶץ מִצְרַיִם" – אֲנִי וְלֹא שָׂרָף. "וּבְכָל אֱלֹהֵי מִצְרַיִם אֶעֱשֶׂה שְׁפָטִים" – אֲנִי וְלֹא הַשָּׁלִיחַ. "אֲנִי יְיָ" – אֲנִי הוּא וְלֹא אַחֵר.

"WITH A STRONG HAND" refers to an epidemic of animal disease (dever) – the fifth plague. *"The **hand** of Adonai will strike your livestock in the fields – the horses, the donkeys, the camels, the cattle, and the sheep – with a very severe disease"* (Ex. 9:3).

"בְּיָד חֲזָקָה." זוֹ הַדֶּבֶר. כְּמָה שֶׁנֶּאֱמַר (שמות ט, ג):
"הִנֵּה יַד יְיָ הוֹיָה, בְּמִקְנְךָ אֲשֶׁר בַּשָּׂדֶה, בַּסּוּסִים בַּחֲמֹרִים בַּגְּמַלִּים, בַּבָּקָר וּבַצֹּאן, דֶּבֶר כָּבֵד מְאֹד."

An Outstretched Arm

וּבִזְרֹעַ נְטוּיָה

According to *an Afghani Jewish custom, the leader of the Seder raises the bone (zeroa) from the seder plate as a symbol of God's outstretched arm (zeroa).*

Kadesh
Urchatz
Karpas
Yachatz
Maggid

Ten
Plagues

"WITH AN OUTSTRETCHED ARM" (zeroa) – refers to God's sword (as a metaphor for the plague of the first born) just as it does elsewhere: *"David woke up and saw the angel of Adonai standing between heaven and earth, with a drawn sword in his hand, outstretched against Jerusalem"* (I Chronicles 21:16).

"וּבִזְרֹעַ נְטוּיָה." זוֹ הַחֶרֶב. כְּמָה שֶׁנֶּאֱמַר (שמות כא, טז): "וְחַרְבּוֹ שְׁלוּפָה בְּיָדוֹ, נְטוּיָה עַל יְרוּשָׁלָיִם."

The Tenth Plague   *by Leon Baxter*

Abraham Lincoln

"If every drop of blood drawn by the lash must be paid by one drawn by the sword, still must it be said, 'The judgments of the Lord are true and righteous altogether.'"
(Psalm. 19; Second Inaugural Address, 1865).

"WITH AWESOME POWER" refers to the revelation of God's power to our very eyes. That is just what Moshe tells Israel: *"Did a God ever before attempt to come and extract one nation for himself from the midst of another nation by prodigious acts, by signs and wonders, by war, by a strong hand, an outstretched arm and awesome power, as Adonai your God did for you in Egypt before your very eyes?"* (Deut. 4:34).

"וּבְמֹרָא גָּדוֹל." זֶה גִּלּוּי שְׁכִינָה. כְּמָה שֶׁנֶּאֱמַר (דברים ד, יז): "אוֹ הֲנִסָּה אֱלֹהִים, לָבוֹא לָקַחַת לוֹ גוֹי מִקֶּרֶב גּוֹי, בְּמַסֹּת בְּאֹתֹת וּבְמוֹפְתִים וּבְמִלְחָמָה, וּבְיָד חֲזָקָה וּבִזְרוֹעַ נְטוּיָה, וּבְמוֹרָאִים גְּדֹלִים. כְּכֹל אֲשֶׁר עָשָׂה לָכֶם יְיָ אֱלֹהֵיכֶם בְּמִצְרַיִם, לְעֵינֶיךָ."

"WITH SIGNS" refers to the staff, as God told Moshe: *"Take the staff in your hand to do signs with it"* (Ex. 4:17).

"וּבְאֹתוֹת." זֶה הַמַּטֶּה, כְּמָה שֶׁנֶּאֱמַר (שמות ד, יז): "וְאֶת הַמַּטֶּה הַזֶּה תִּקַּח בְּיָדֶךָ, אֲשֶׁר תַּעֲשֶׂה בּוֹ אֶת הָאֹתֹת."

God's Finger and the Sixteen Drops

אֶצְבַּע אֱלֹהִים

It is a medieval custom to dip one's finger in the Seder's second cup of wine and to remove sixteen drops of wine. As each plague is recited we decrease our own joy, drop by drop, as we recall the enemy's pain. Besides the **ten plagues**, the extra six drops correspond to the three prophetic plagues mentioned by the prophet Joel – **blood, fire and smoke** – and the three word abbreviation of the ten plagues invented by Rabbi Yehuda – **d'tzach, adash, b'achab.**

"WITH WONDERS" refers to the plagues of blood, fire and smoke that are recalled by the prophet Joel: "Before the great and terrible day of Adonai comes, I will set wonders in the sky and on earth . . . **blood, fire, pillars of smoke! Da-am** (drop of wine) **va-eish** (drop) **v'teemrot ashan** (drop)! The sun shall turn to darkness and the moon into blood" *(Joel 3:3).*

"וּבְמוֹפְתִים." זֶה הַדָּם. כְּמָה שֶׁנֶּאֱמַר (יואל ג, ג):

"וְנָתַתִּי מוֹפְתִים,
בַּשָּׁמַיִם וּבָאָרֶץ:

דָּם.
וָאֵשׁ.
וְתִימְרוֹת עָשָׁן."

דָּבָר אַחֵר.
"בְּיָד חֲזָקָה"   שְׁתַּיִם.
"וּבִזְרֹעַ נְטוּיָה"   שְׁתַּיִם.
"וּבְמֹרָא גָּדוֹל"   שְׁתַּיִם.
"וּבְאֹתוֹת"   שְׁתַּיִם.
"וּבְמֹפְתִים"   שְׁתַּיִם.

Pharaoh's Frogs

one morning when Pharaoh woke in his bed,
there were frogs in his bed, and...
frogs on his head,
frogs on his nose,
and frogs on his toes,
frogs HERE frogs THERE
frogs were jumping EVERYWHERE!

Otto Geismar, 1927

Recount the Plagues

Recount the plagues that have struck this year and for each remove a drop of wine from one's cup of joy. Some families recount ecological, economic or political plagues at this point.

The Ten Plagues

עֶשֶׂר מַכּוֹת

The Holy One Blessed Be He brought
ten plagues on the Egyptians in Egypt.
These are the ten:

אֵלּוּ עֶשֶׂר מַכּוֹת שֶׁהֵבִיא
הַקָּדוֹשׁ בָּרוּךְ הוּא עַל
הַמִּצְרִים בְּמִצְרַיִם, וְאֵלּוּ הֵן:

Kadesh
Urchatz
Karpas
Yachatz
Maggid

Ten
Plagues

Blood	1. דָּם
Frogs	2. צְפַרְדֵּעַ
Lice	3. כִּנִּים
Wild beasts (or insects)	4. עָרוֹב
Cattle plague	5. דֶּבֶר
Boils	6. שְׁחִין
Hail	7. בָּרָד
Locust	8. אַרְבֶּה
Darkness	9. חֹשֶׁךְ
Death of the Firstborn	10. מַכַּת בְּכוֹרוֹת

Rabbi Yehuda used to abbreviate them as an acrostic :

רַבִּי יְהוּדָה הָיָה נוֹתֵן בָּהֶם סִמָנִים:

D-Tza-Kh *(drop)*   *(Da-am/Tzefar-dei-ah/Kee-neem)*   דְּצַ"ךְ

A-Da-Sh *(drop)*   *(Ah-rov/Deh-ver/Sh'cheen)*   עַדַ"שׁ

B'-A-Cha-B *(drop)*   *(Ba-rad/Ar-beh/Cho-shech/Makat B'chorot)*   בְּאַחַ"ב.

250 מַכּוֹת

רַבִּי יוֹסֵי הַגְּלִילִי אוֹמֵר: מִנַּיִן אַתָּה אוֹמֵר, שֶׁלָּקוּ הַמִּצְרִים בְּמִצְרַיִם עֶשֶׂר מַכּוֹת, וְעַל הַיָּם, לָקוּ חֲמִשִּׁים מַכּוֹת?

בְּמִצְרַיִם מָה הוּא אוֹמֵר: "וַיֹּאמְרוּ הַחַרְטֻמִּם אֶל פַּרְעֹה, אֶצְבַּע אֱלֹהִים הוּא" (שמות ח, טז).

וְעַל הַיָּם מָה הוּא אוֹמֵר? "וַיַּרְא יִשְׂרָאֵל אֶת הַיָּד הַגְּדֹלָה, אֲשֶׁר עָשָׂה יְיָ בְּמִצְרַיִם, וַיִּירְאוּ הָעָם אֶת יְיָ. וַיַּאֲמִינוּ בַּייָ, וּבְמשֶׁה עַבְדּוֹ" (שמות יד, לא). כַּמָּה לָקוּ בְּאֶצְבַּע – עֶשֶׂר מַכּוֹת. אֱמֹר מֵעַתָּה, בְּמִצְרַיִם לָקוּ עֶשֶׂר מַכּוֹת, וְעַל הַיָּם, לָקוּ חֲמִשִּׁים מַכּוֹת.

רַבִּי אֱלִיעֶזֶר אוֹמֵר: מִנַּיִן שֶׁכָּל מַכָּה וּמַכָּה, שֶׁהֵבִיא הַקָּדוֹשׁ בָּרוּךְ הוּא עַל הַמִּצְרִים בְּמִצְרַיִם, הָיְתָה שֶׁל אַרְבַּע מַכּוֹת?

שֶׁנֶּאֱמַר (תהילים עח, מט): "יְשַׁלַּח בָּם חֲרוֹן אַפּוֹ, עֶבְרָה וָזַעַם וְצָרָה. מִשְׁלַחַת מַלְאֲכֵי רָעִים." עֶבְרָה אַחַת. וָזַעַם שְׁתַּיִם. וְצָרָה שָׁלֹשׁ. מִשְׁלַחַת מַלְאֲכֵי רָעִים אַרְבַּע. אֱמֹר מֵעַתָּה, בְּמִצְרַיִם לָקוּ אַרְבָּעִים מַכּוֹת, וְעַל הַיָּם לָקוּ מָאתַיִם מַכּוֹת.

רַבִּי עֲקִיבָא אוֹמֵר: מִנַּיִן שֶׁכָּל מַכָּה וּמַכָּה, שֶׁהֵבִיא הַקָּדוֹשׁ בָּרוּךְ הוּא עַל הַמִּצְרִים בְּמִצְרַיִם, הָיְתָה שֶׁל חָמֵשׁ מַכּוֹת?

שֶׁנֶּאֱמַר: "יְשַׁלַּח בָּם חֲרוֹן אַפּוֹ, עֶבְרָה וָזַעַם וְצָרָה. מִשְׁלַחַת מַלְאֲכֵי רָעִים." חֲרוֹן אַפּוֹ אַחַת. עֶבְרָה שְׁתַּיִם. וָזַעַם שָׁלֹשׁ. וְצָרָה אַרְבַּע. מִשְׁלַחַת מַלְאֲכֵי רָעִים חָמֵשׁ. אֱמֹר מֵעַתָּה, בְּמִצְרַיִם לָקוּ חֲמִשִּׁים מַכּוֹת, וְעַל הַיָּם לָקוּ חֲמִשִּׁים וּמָאתַיִם מַכּוֹת.

"Let My People Go" *An African-American Spiritual*

When Israel was in Egypt's land,
"Let My people go" *(Ex. 5:1)*.
Oppressed so hard they could not stand,
"Let My people go."

Go down, Moses,
way down in Egypt's land,
Tell old Pharaoh: "Let My people go."

Thus said the Lord, bold Moses said,
"Let My people go."
If not, I'll smite your first-born dead,
"Let My people go."

Go down, Moses,
way down in Egypt's land,
Tell old Pharaoh: "Let My people go."

No more shall they in bondage toil,
"Let My people go."
Let them come out with Egypt's spoil,
"Let My people go."

Go down, Moses,
way down in Egypt's land,
Tell old Pharaoh: "Let My people go."

Dayeinu
"It Would Have Been Enough"

דַּיֵּנוּ

Dayeinu commemorates a long list of miraculous things God did for us, any one of which would have been pretty amazing just by itself. For example, "Had God only taken us out of Egypt but not punished the Egyptians – it would have been enough." **Dayeinu**, translated liberally, means, "Thank you, God, for overdoing it." (See the English on page 51).

(See the English on page 51).

Kadesh
Urchatz
Karpas
Yachatz
Maggid

Dayeinu

כַּמָּה מַעֲלוֹת טוֹבוֹת לַמָּקוֹם עָלֵינוּ:

אִלּוּ הוֹצִיאָנוּ מִמִּצְרַיִם,
וְלֹא עָשָׂה בָהֶם שְׁפָטִים, **דַּיֵּנוּ!**

אִלּוּ עָשָׂה בָהֶם שְׁפָטִים,
וְלֹא עָשָׂה בֵאלֹהֵיהֶם, **דַּיֵּנוּ!**

אִלּוּ עָשָׂה בֵאלֹהֵיהֶם,
וְלֹא הָרַג אֶת בְּכוֹרֵיהֶם, **דַּיֵּנוּ!**

אִלּוּ הָרַג אֶת בְּכוֹרֵיהֶם,
וְלֹא נָתַן לָנוּ אֶת מָמוֹנָם, **דַּיֵּנוּ!**

אִלּוּ נָתַן לָנוּ אֶת מָמוֹנָם,
וְלֹא קָרַע לָנוּ אֶת הַיָּם, **דַּיֵּנוּ!**

Ee-lu ho-tzee-anu mee-Meetz-ra-yeem,
v'lo asa va-hem sh'fa-teem, **Da-yeinu**

Ee-lu asa va-hem sh'fa-teem,
v'lo asa vei-lo-hei-hem, **Da-yeinu**

Ee-lu asa vei-lo-hei-hem,
v'lo ha-rag et b'cho-rei-hem, **Da-yeinu**

Ee-lu ha-rag et b'cho-rei-hem,
v'lo natan la-nu et ma-mo-nam, **Da-yeinu**

Ee-lu natan la-nu et ma-mo-nam,
v'lo kara la-nu et ha-yam, **Da-yeinu**

48

אִלּוּ קָרַע לָנוּ אֶת הַיָּם,
וְלֹא הֶעֱבִירָנוּ בְּתוֹכוֹ בֶּחָרָבָה, דַּיֵּנוּ!

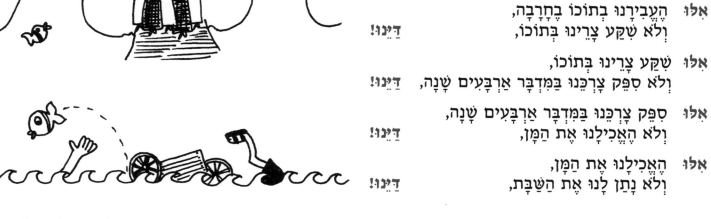

אִלּוּ הֶעֱבִירָנוּ בְּתוֹכוֹ בֶּחָרָבָה,
וְלֹא שִׁקַּע צָרֵינוּ בְּתוֹכוֹ, דַּיֵּנוּ!

אִלּוּ שִׁקַּע צָרֵינוּ בְּתוֹכוֹ,
וְלֹא סִפֵּק צָרְכֵּנוּ בַּמִּדְבָּר אַרְבָּעִים שָׁנָה, דַּיֵּנוּ!

אִלּוּ סִפֵּק צָרְכֵּנוּ בַּמִּדְבָּר אַרְבָּעִים שָׁנָה,
וְלֹא הֶאֱכִילָנוּ אֶת הַמָּן, דַּיֵּנוּ!

אִלּוּ הֶאֱכִילָנוּ אֶת הַמָּן,
וְלֹא נָתַן לָנוּ אֶת הַשַּׁבָּת, דַּיֵּנוּ!

Ee-lu ka-ra la-nu et ha-yam,
v'lo he-eh-vee-ra-nu
v'to-cho beh-cha-ra-va, **Da-yeinu**

Ee-lu he-eh-vee-ra-nu
b'to-cho beh-cha-ra-va,
v'lo shee-ka et tza-rei-nu b'to-cho, **Da-yeinu**

Ee-lu shee-ka et tza-rei-nu b'to-cho,
v'lo see-peik tzor-kei-nu ba-meed-bar
ar-ba-eem shana, **Da-yeinu**

Ee-lu see-peik tzor-kei-nu ba-meed-bar
ar-ba-eem sha-na,
v'lo he-eh-chee-la-nu et ha-man, **Da-yeinu**

Ee-lu he-eh-chee-la-nu et ha-man,
v'lo na-tan la-nu et ha-Shabbat **Da-yeinu**

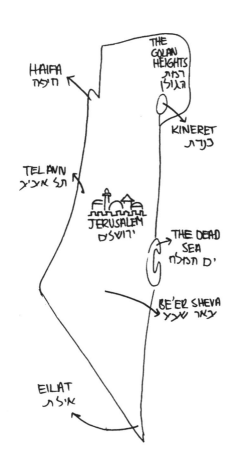

The Afghani Onion Free-for-All

If things at your Seder are slowing down and people seem drowsy, try the Afghani custom of distributing green onions.

Beginning with the ninth stanza, *"Even if You had supplied our needs in the desert for 40 years, but not fed us manna from heaven,"* the participants hit each other (gently?) with the green onion stalks, everytime they sing the refrain *"Da-yeinu."* (See explanation of custom in unabridged A Different Night, p. 107.)

אִלוּ נָתַן לָנוּ אֶת הַשַּׁבָּת,
וְלֹא קֵרְבָנוּ לִפְנֵי הַר סִינַי, דַּיֵּנוּ!

אִלוּ קֵרְבָנוּ לִפְנֵי הַר סִינַי,
וְלֹא נָתַן לָנוּ אֶת הַתּוֹרָה, דַּיֵּנוּ!

אִלוּ נָתַן לָנוּ אֶת הַתּוֹרָה,
וְלֹא הִכְנִיסָנוּ לְאֶרֶץ יִשְׂרָאֵל, דַּיֵּנוּ!

אִלוּ הִכְנִיסָנוּ לְאֶרֶץ יִשְׂרָאֵל,
וְלֹא בָנָה לָנוּ אֶת בֵּית הַבְּחִירָה, דַּיֵּנוּ!

Kadesh
Urchatz
Karpas
Yachatz
Maggid

Dayeinu

Ee-lu	na-tan la-nu et ha-Shabbat ,	
	v'lo ker-va-nu leef-nei har See-nai,	**Da-yeinu**
Ee-lu	ker-va-nu leef-nei har See-nai,	
	v'lo na-tan la-nu et ha-Torah,	**Da-yeinu**
Ee-lu	na-tan la-nu et ha-Torah,	
	v'lo heech-nee-sa-nu l'Eretz Yisrael,	**Da-yeinu**
Ee-lu	heech-nee-sa-nu l'Eretz Yisrael,	
	v'lo va-na la-nu et beit ha-b'chee-ra,	**Da-yeinu**

Dayeinu Continued

עַל אַחַת כַּמָּה וְכַמָּה

EACH ONE of these good things would have been enough to earn our thanks. Dayeinu!

GOD took us out of Egypt, punished the oppressors, and humiliated their gods, exposing their futility.

GOD killed their first born (when the Egyptians refused to release Israel, God's first born) and gave us some of the Egyptians' wealth, just compensation for our labor.

GOD divided the Red Sea for us, bringing us across on dry land, while drowning our pursuers in the sea.

GOD supplied our needs for forty years in the desert – feeding us manna.

GOD granted us the Shabbat and brought us to Mount Sinai to receive the Torah.

GOD ushered us into Eretz Yisrael and later built us a Temple, the chosen place to atone for our crimes and misdemeanors.

Recounting Our Blessings: An Update

Dayeinu establishes a pattern of enumerating our blessings on Pesach. However it ends with the building of the Temple circa 1000 B.C.E.

Suggest another ten national or family events deserving thanks since 1000 B.C.E. Recall, – for example, the Six Day War (1967), or the airlift of Ethiopian Jews to Israel (1991), or the birth of a long-awaited child.

עַל אַחַת כַּמָּה וְכַמָּה טוֹבָה כְפוּלָה
וּמְכֻפֶּלֶת לַמָּקוֹם עָלֵינוּ:

שֶׁהוֹצִיאָנוּ מִמִּצְרַיִם,
וְעָשָׂה בָהֶם שְׁפָטִים,
וְעָשָׂה בֵאלֹהֵיהֶם,

וְהָרַג אֶת בְּכוֹרֵיהֶם,
וְנָתַן לָנוּ אֶת מָמוֹנָם,

וְקָרַע לָנוּ אֶת הַיָּם,
וְהֶעֱבִירָנוּ בְּתוֹכוֹ בֶּחָרָבָה,
וְשִׁקַּע צָרֵינוּ בְּתוֹכוֹ,

וְסִפֵּק צָרְכֵּנוּ בַּמִּדְבָּר אַרְבָּעִים שָׁנָה,
וְהֶאֱכִילָנוּ אֶת הַמָּן,

וְנָתַן לָנוּ אֶת הַשַּׁבָּת,
וְקֵרְבָנוּ לִפְנֵי הַר סִינַי, וְנָתַן לָנוּ אֶת הַתּוֹרָה,

וְהִכְנִיסָנוּ לְאֶרֶץ יִשְׂרָאֵל,
וּבָנָה לָנוּ אֶת בֵּית הַבְּחִירָה,
לְכַפֵּר עַל כָּל עֲוֹנוֹתֵינוּ.

Otto Geismar 1927

Pesach, Matza and Maror

פֶּסַח, מַצָּה, וּמָרוֹר

1. *The Maggid* section (devoted to storytelling and explanations) is almost complete. Before eating the Seder's edible symbols, the Haggadah brings us **Rabban Gamliel's checklist** on the three essential foods, whose significance must be understood by all the participants in the Seder.

Why these three? The Pesach lamb, matza and maror constituted the original menu in the Egyptian Seder. "They shall eat the meat (of the lamb) . . . roasted over the fire, with matza and with maror" (Ex. 12:8).

2. *As in* a three act play Rabban Gamliel identifies these foods with three progressive historical moments in the Exodus:
(1) **Maror** captures the bitterness of the enslavement;
(2) The **Pesach lamb**, represented today by the roasted bone (zeroa), recalls the blood on the doorposts and the terror and anticipation of the night of the plague of the first born;
(3) **Matza** stands for the following morning, when Israel was rushed out of Egypt with no time to let their dough rise.

Kadesh
Urchatz
Karpas
Yachatz
Maggid

Rabban Gamliel

RABBAN GAMLIEL used to say: "All who have not explained the significance of three things during the Pesach Seder have not yet fulfilled their duty. The three are: the **Pesach lamb**, the **matza** and the **maror**."

WHY THE PESACH LAMB?

Leader points at (but does not raise) the roasted bone:
"Pesach Al Shum Ma?" – The **Passover lamb** (that our ancestors ate in the days of the Temple) – why did we used to eat it?

All:

TO REMIND ourselves that God **passed over** our ancestors' houses in Egypt (at this very hour on this very date). Moshe has already instructed us: *"When your children ask you, 'What do you mean by this ceremony?' you shall say: 'It is the Passover offering to Adonai, because God passed over the houses of Israel in Egypt when God struck the Egyptians, but saved our houses . . . .'"* (Ex. 12:26-27).

רַבָּן גַּמְלִיאֵל הָיָה אוֹמֵר: כָּל שֶׁלֹּא אָמַר שְׁלֹשָׁה דְבָרִים אֵלּוּ בַּפֶּסַח, לֹא יָצָא יְדֵי חוֹבָתוֹ, וְאֵלּוּ הֵן: פֶּסַח, מַצָּה, וּמָרוֹר.

פֶּסַח שֶׁהָיוּ
אֲבוֹתֵינוּ אוֹכְלִים,
בִּזְמַן שֶׁבֵּית
הַמִּקְדָּשׁ הָיָה קַיָּם,
עַל שׁוּם מָה?

*Arye Allweil, 1949
(first Israeli army Haggadah)*

עַל שׁוּם שֶׁפָּסַח הַקָּדוֹשׁ בָּרוּךְ הוּא, עַל בָּתֵּי אֲבוֹתֵינוּ בְּמִצְרַיִם, שֶׁנֶּאֱמַר (שמות יב, כז): "וַאֲמַרְתֶּם זֶבַח פֶּסַח הוּא לַיְיָ, אֲשֶׁר פָּסַח עַל בָּתֵּי בְנֵי יִשְׂרָאֵל בְּמִצְרַיִם בְּנָגְפּוֹ אֶת מִצְרַיִם, וְאֶת בָּתֵּינוּ הִצִּיל. וַיִּקֹּד הָעָם וַיִּשְׁתַּחֲווּ."

Why This Matza?

מַצָּה עַל שׁוּם מַה?

Everyone holds up matza.

Leader:

"Matza Al Shum Ma?" – This matza! Why do we eat it?

מַצָּה זוֹ שֶׁאָנוּ אוֹכְלִים, עַל שׁוּם מַה?

All:

TO REMIND ourselves that even before the dough of our ancestors in Egypt had time to rise and become leavened, the King of kings, the Holy One Blessed be He, revealed Himself and redeemed them.
The Torah says: *"They baked unleavened cakes of the dough that they had taken out of Egypt, for it was not leavened, since they had been driven out of Egypt and could not delay; nor had they prepared any provisions for themselves"* (Ex. 12:39).

עַל שׁוּם שֶׁלֹּא הִסְפִּיק בְּצֵקָם שֶׁל אֲבוֹתֵינוּ לְהַחֲמִיץ, עַד שֶׁנִּגְלָה עֲלֵיהֶם מֶלֶךְ מַלְכֵי הַמְּלָכִים, הַקָּדוֹשׁ בָּרוּךְ הוּא, וּגְאָלָם, שֶׁנֶּאֱמַר (שמות יב, לט): "וַיֹּאפוּ אֶת הַבָּצֵק, אֲשֶׁר הוֹצִיאוּ מִמִּצְרַיִם, עֻגֹת מַצּוֹת, כִּי לֹא חָמֵץ. כִּי גֹרְשׁוּ מִמִּצְרַיִם, וְלֹא יָכְלוּ לְהִתְמַהְמֵהַּ, וְגַם צֵדָה לֹא עָשׂוּ לָהֶם."

Why This Maror?

מָרוֹר עַל שׁוּם מַה?

Everyone raises maror from the Seder plate.

Leader:

"Maror Al Shum Ma?" – This maror! Why do we eat it?

מָרוֹר זֶה שֶׁאָנוּ אוֹכְלִים, עַל שׁוּם מַה?

All:

TO REMIND ourselves that the Egyptians embittered our ancestors' lives: *"They embittered their lives with hard labor, with mortar and bricks (construction) and with all sorts of field labor (agriculture). Whatever the task, they worked them ruthlessly"* (Ex 1:14).

עַל שׁוּם שֶׁמֵּרְרוּ הַמִּצְרִים אֶת חַיֵּי אֲבוֹתֵינוּ בְּמִצְרַיִם, שֶׁנֶּאֱמַר (שמות א, יד): "וַיְמָרְרוּ אֶת חַיֵּיהֶם בַּעֲבֹדָה קָשָׁה, בְּחֹמֶר וּבִלְבֵנִים, וּבְכָל עֲבֹדָה בַּשָּׂדֶה. אֵת כָּל עֲבֹדָתָם, אֲשֶׁר עָבְדוּ בָהֶם בְּפָרֶךְ."

In Every Generation

בְּכָל דּוֹר וָדוֹר

Identifying with the Exodus
"The Exodus from Egypt occurs in every human being, in every era, in every year and even on every day," said the Hassidic Rabbi Nachman of Bratslav. At the Seder we must try to empathize with that original liberation and discover its relevance throughout the generations.

Kadesh
Urchatz
Karpas
Yachatz
Maggid

In Every Generation
Hallel Begins

IN EVERY generation one is obligated to see oneself as one who personally went out from Egypt. Just as it says: *"You shall tell your child on that very day: 'It's because of this that God did for **me** when **I went out from Egypt'"** (Ex. 13:8).

NOT ONLY were our ancestors redeemed by the Holy One Blessed Be He, but even **we** were redeemed with them. Just as it says: *"God took **us** out from there in order to bring **us** and to give **us** the land God swore to our ancestors"* (Deut. 6:23).

בְּכָל דּוֹר וָדוֹר חַיָּב אָדָם לִרְאוֹת אֶת עַצְמוֹ,
כְּאִלּוּ הוּא יָצָא מִמִּצְרָיִם.
שֶׁנֶּאֱמַר (שמות יב, ח): "וְהִגַּדְתָּ לְבִנְךָ בַּיּוֹם הַהוּא לֵאמֹר:
בַּעֲבוּר זֶה עָשָׂה יְיָ לִי, בְּצֵאתִי מִמִּצְרָיִם."

לֹא אֶת אֲבוֹתֵינוּ בִּלְבָד, גָּאַל הַקָּדוֹשׁ בָּרוּךְ הוּא,
אֶלָּא אַף אוֹתָנוּ גָּאַל עִמָּהֶם, שֶׁנֶּאֱמַר (דברים ו, כג):
"וְאוֹתָנוּ הוֹצִיא מִשָּׁם, לְמַעַן הָבִיא אֹתָנוּ, לָתֶת לָנוּ
אֶת הָאָרֶץ אֲשֶׁר נִשְׁבַּע לַאֲבֹתֵינוּ."

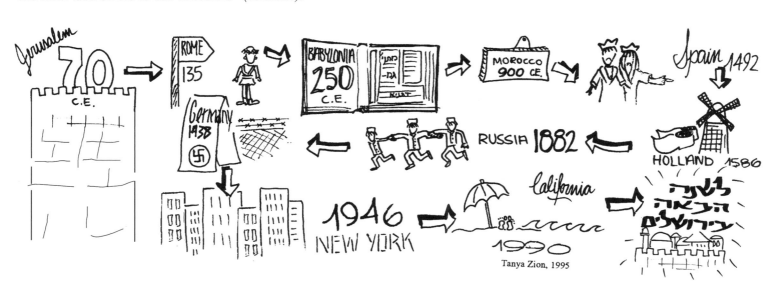

Tanya Zion, 1995

A New Song – Hallel-u-jah

After covering all the matza at the table, everyone raises their second cup of wine in a toast to God and sings Hallel.

לְפִיכָךְ

Ben Shahn,
Hallelujah Suite,
© 1996 Ben Shahn/Vaga, NY

Leader: **WE HAVE** just completed the Maggid, the
story that begins with slavery and ends with liberation.
We have retold it as our own personal story.
Now it is only fitting that we thank God
by singing a new song.

THEREFORE we owe it to God: to thank, to sing,
to praise and honor, to glorify and bless,
to raise up and acclaim the One who has done all
these wonders for our ancestors and for us.

God took us from **slavery to freedom**,
    from **sorrow to joy**,
    from **mourning to festivity**,
    from **thick darkness to a great light**,
    from **enslavement to redemption**!
Let us sing before God, a new song. **HALLELUJAH!**

לְפִיכָךְ אֲנַחְנוּ חַיָּבִים לְהוֹדוֹת, לְהַלֵּל, לְשַׁבֵּחַ,
לְפָאֵר, לְרוֹמֵם, לְהַדֵּר, לְבָרֵךְ, לְעַלֵּה וּלְקַלֵּס,
לְמִי שֶׁעָשָׂה לַאֲבוֹתֵינוּ וְלָנוּ אֶת כָּל הַנִּסִים הָאֵלוּ.

הוֹצִיאָנוּ מֵעַבְדוּת לְחֵרוּת, מִיָּגוֹן לְשִׂמְחָה,
וּמֵאֵבֶל לְיוֹם טוֹב, וּמֵאֲפֵלָה לְאוֹר גָּדוֹל,
וּמִשִּׁעְבּוּד לִגְאֻלָּה.
וְנֹאמַר לְפָנָיו שִׁירָה חֲדָשָׁה. הַלְלוּיָהּ.

My Narrow Prison

*The Hebrew word for Egypt, "Meetzrayim,"
means a tight spot or a narrow strait
where we feel "boxed in."*

One day, a few days after the liberation, I walked through the country past flowering meadows, for miles and miles, toward the market town near the camp.

Larks rose to the sky and I could hear their joyous song. There was no one to be seen for miles around; there was nothing but the wide earth and sky and the larks' jubilation and the **freedom of space**. I stopped, looked around, and up to the sky – and then I went down on my knees. At that moment there was very little I knew of myself or of the world – I had but one sentence in mind – always

the same: *"I called to Adonai from my narrow prison and God answered me in the freedom of space"* (Psalm 118:5).

How long I knelt there and repeated this sentence, memory can no longer recall. But I know that on that day, in that hour, my new life started. Step for step I progressed, until I again became a human being.

(Viktor Frankl, Man's Search for Meaning, lessons from a concentration camp)

Hallel: Psalm 113

הַלֵּל

The first part of Hallel (Psalms 113-114) begins here before the meal and the rest is completed after eating. The verses which we have printed in bold stand out as particularly relevant to the Exodus when recited on Passover.

הַלְלוּיָהּ.
הַלְלוּ עַבְדֵי יְיָ. הַלְלוּ אֶת שֵׁם יְיָ.
יְהִי שֵׁם יְיָ מְבֹרָךְ מֵעַתָּה וְעַד עוֹלָם.
מִמִּזְרַח שֶׁמֶשׁ עַד מְבוֹאוֹ מְהֻלָּל שֵׁם יְיָ.
רָם עַל כָּל גּוֹיִם יְיָ, עַל הַשָּׁמַיִם כְּבוֹדוֹ.
מִי כַּיְיָ אֱלֹהֵינוּ, הַמַּגְבִּיהִי לָשָׁבֶת.
הַמַּשְׁפִּילִי לִרְאוֹת בַּשָּׁמַיִם וּבָאָרֶץ.
מְקִימִי מֵעָפָר דָּל, מֵאַשְׁפֹּת יָרִים אֶבְיוֹן.
לְהוֹשִׁיבִי עִם נְדִיבִים, עִם נְדִיבֵי עַמּוֹ.
מוֹשִׁיבִי עֲקֶרֶת הַבַּיִת, אֵם הַבָּנִים שְׂמֵחָה.
הַלְלוּיָהּ.

Kadesh
Urchatz
Karpas
Yachatz
Maggid

Hallel
Begins

"When I Went Out"

Israeli Minister NATAN SHARANSKY (former Prisoner of Zion) writes:

"I, as practically all Soviet Jews, was absolutely assimilated. I knew nothing about our language, about our history, about our religion. But the pride of being a Jew, the pride for our State of Israel after the Six Day War, made me feel free. And, after I turned to Jewish identification, I felt myself really free from that big Soviet prison. I was free even before the very last day of my leaving the Soviet Union."

VLADIMIR SLEPAK described his first Israeli morning: "It is like being reborn. Until I die, I'll never forget this morning, when I woke up and looked out at the sun rising over the Judean Hills, and the Old City in front of me."

IDA NUDEL said upon arrival at Ben Gurion Airport: "A few hours ago I was almost a slave in Moscow. Now I'm a free woman in my own country. It is the most important moment of my life. I am at home at the soul of the Jewish people. I am a free person among my own people" *(from the CLAL Soviet Jewry Haggadah).*

HALLELUJAH.
 Servants of Adonai, give praise;
 praise the name of Adonai.
Let the name of Adonai be blessed now and forever.
From east to west the name of Adonai is praised.
 Adonai is exalted above all nations;
 God's glory is above the heavens.
Who is like Adonai our God,
who, enthroned on high,
sees what is below, in heaven and on earth?
 God raises the poor from the dust,
 lifts up the needy from the refuse heap
 to place them with the great men of God's people.
God places the childless woman among her household
as a happy mother of children.
HALLELUJAH.

Hallel: Psalm 114

בְּצֵאת יִשְׂרָאֵל

בְּצֵאת יִשְׂרָאֵל מִמִּצְרָיִם בֵּית יַעֲקֹב מֵעַם לֹעֵז.
הָיְתָה יְהוּדָה לְקָדְשׁוֹ יִשְׂרָאֵל מַמְשְׁלוֹתָיו.
הַיָּם רָאָה וַיָּנֹס הַיַּרְדֵּן יִסֹּב לְאָחוֹר.
הֶהָרִים רָקְדוּ כְאֵילִים גְּבָעוֹת כִּבְנֵי צֹאן.
מַה לְּךָ הַיָּם כִּי תָנוּס הַיַּרְדֵּן תִּסֹּב לְאָחוֹר.
הֶהָרִים תִּרְקְדוּ כְאֵילִים גְּבָעוֹת כִּבְנֵי צֹאן.
מִלִּפְנֵי אָדוֹן חוּלִי אָרֶץ מִלִּפְנֵי אֱלוֹהַּ יַעֲקֹב.
הַהֹפְכִי הַצּוּר אֲגַם מָיִם חַלָּמִישׁ לְמַעְיְנוֹ מָיִם.

WHEN ISRAEL went forth from Egypt,
The house of Jacob from a people of strange speech,
>   Judah became God's holy one,
>   Israel, God's dominion.

The sea saw them and fled,
The Jordan ran backward,
>   Mountains skipped like rams,
>   Hills like sheep.

What alarmed you, sea, that you fled,
Jordan, that you ran backward,
>   Mountains, that you skipped like rams,
>   Hills, like sheep?

Tremble, earth,
at the presence of Adonai,
at the presence of
the God of Jacob,
>   Who turned the rock
>   into a pool of water,
>   The flinty rock
>   into a fountain.

Ben Shahn, Hallelujah Suite

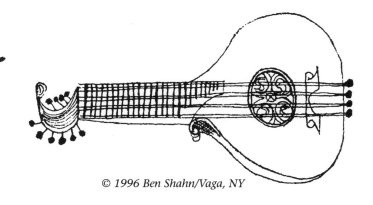

© 1996 Ben Shahn/Vaga, NY

When NOT to Sing

1. "If your enemy falls, do not celebrate.
If he trips, let not your heart rejoice" *(Proverbs 24:17).*

2. Rabbi Yochanan
"God is not happy at the downfall of the wicked. . . . When the angels tried to sing songs of praise to God at the Red Sea, God silenced them: **'My handiwork, my human creatures, are drowning in the sea and you want to sing a song of praise?'**" *(T.B. Megillah 10b).*

The Cup of Redemption

כּוֹס שֵׁנִי

1. **We conclude** the long Maggid section (storytelling) by drinking the second cup of wine, the Cup of Redemption.

2. **Recline** on a pillow to the left and drink at least half the second cup of wine.

HERE I AM, ready to perform the mitzvah of the second of the four cups, the cup of redemption.

הִנְנִי מוּכָן וּמְזֻמָּן לְקַיֵּם מִצְוַת כּוֹס שֵׁנִי שֶׁל אַרְבַּע כּוֹסוֹת.

BLESSED ARE YOU, Adonai our God, Ruler of the Universe, who redeemed us and redeemed our ancestors from Egypt, and who brought us to this night to eat matza and maror. Adonai, our God and God of our ancestors, may You bring us in peace to future holidays. May we celebrate them in your rebuilt city, and may we be able to eat the Pesach lamb and the other sacrifices offered on the altar. We will thank you for our redemption. BLESSED ARE YOU, the Redeemer of Israel.

בָּרוּךְ אַתָּה יְיָ, אֱלֹהֵינוּ מֶלֶךְ הָעוֹלָם, אֲשֶׁר גְּאָלָנוּ וְגָאַל אֶת אֲבוֹתֵינוּ מִמִּצְרַיִם, וְהִגִּיעָנוּ לַלַּיְלָה הַזֶּה, לֶאֱכָל בּוֹ מַצָּה וּמָרוֹר. כֵּן, יְיָ אֱלֹהֵינוּ וֵאלֹהֵי אֲבוֹתֵינוּ, יַגִּיעֵנוּ לְמוֹעֲדִים וְלִרְגָלִים אֲחֵרִים, הַבָּאִים לִקְרָאתֵנוּ לְשָׁלוֹם, שְׂמֵחִים בְּבִנְיַן עִירֶךָ, וְשָׂשִׂים בַּעֲבוֹדָתֶךָ. וְנֹאכַל שָׁם מִן הַזְּבָחִים וּמִן הַפְּסָחִים, אֲשֶׁר יַגִּיעַ דָּמָם, עַל קִיר מִזְבַּחֲךָ לְרָצוֹן, וְנוֹדֶה לְּךָ שִׁיר חָדָשׁ עַל גְּאֻלָתֵנוּ, וְעַל פְּדוּת נַפְשֵׁנוּ.

בָּרוּךְ אַתָּה יְיָ, גָּאַל יִשְׂרָאֵל.

BLESSED ARE YOU, Adonai our God, Ruler of the Universe, Creator of the Fruit of the Vine.

Ba-ruch ata Adonai, Elo-hei-nu me-lech ha-olam, bo-rei pree ha-gafen.

בָּרוּךְ אַתָּה יְיָ, אֱלֹהֵינוּ מֶלֶךְ הָעוֹלָם, בּוֹרֵא פְּרִי הַגָּפֶן.

Kadesh
Urchatz
Karpas
Yachatz
Maggid
Rachtza
Motzi
Matza

Second Cup

Washing Hands and Eating Matza

Miriam's Cup

Many contemporary women pour water into a large decorative cup in honor of Miriam the heroine and poet/prophet, the singer and dancer, who not only saved baby Moshe from the Nile but led the celebration of redemption at the Red Sea. The water in her cup recalls the Rabbis' identification of Miriam with the legendary "wandering well" that nourished Israel in the desert with its waters of life but it also symbolizes the rebirth of freedom. Sometimes each guest is asked to pour a little water into the Cup of Miriam and to express their wishes for healing and rejuvenation.

Rachatza
Washing Before Eating Matza

רָחְצָה

1. **Finally** we begin the Passover meal, the third section or "third cup" of the Seder. Storytelling leads into communal eating, because on Passover, "Jews eat history."

2. **On Passover** the traditional handwashing is often done seated, while volunteers bring around a pitcher, a towel and a basin to each participant. After pouring water over each hand, say the blessing.

BLESSED ARE YOU, Adonai our God, Ruler of the Universe, who sanctified us with Divine mitzvot and commanded us on the washing of the hands.

Ba-ruch ata Adonai, Elo-hei-nu me-lech ha-olam, asher kee-d'shanu b'meetz-vo-tav v'tzee-va-nu al n'teelat ya-da-yeem.

בָּרוּךְ אַתָּה יְיָ אֱלֹהֵינוּ מֶלֶךְ
הָעוֹלָם, אֲשֶׁר קִדְּשָׁנוּ
בְּמִצְוֹתָיו, וְצִוָּנוּ
עַל נְטִילַת יָדָיִם.

Motzi/Matza
Eating the Matza

מוֹצִיא/מַצָּה

1. **This is the one time** during Pesach in which one is obligated to eat matza. (It must be plain matza without eggs or other ingredients that might enrich this bread of poverty).
   Take the three matzot in hand. Make sure the middle one is broken and the others are still whole. Recite the usual blessing for all forms of bread – the "motzi" – and the special blessing for matza – "al acheelat matza."

2. **Take and eat** from the top and middle matza, while reclining (left). Save the third matza for the Hillel sandwich.
   You may dip the matza in salt or charoset.
   Some rabbis require that one eat an amount equivalent to at least 1/2 - 2/3 of a standard machine-made matza.

HERE I AM, ready to perform the mitzvah of eating matza.

הִנְנִי מוּכָן וּמְזֻמָּן לְקַיֵּם מִצְוַת אֲכִילַת מָרוֹר.

BLESSED ARE YOU, Adonai our God, Ruler of the Universe, who extracts bread from the earth.

Ba-ruch ata Adonai, Elo-hei-nu me-lech ha-olam, ha-mo-tzee le-chem meen ha-aretz.

בָּרוּךְ אַתָּה יְיָ, אֱלֹהֵינוּ
מֶלֶךְ הָעוֹלָם, הַמּוֹצִיא
לֶחֶם מִן הָאָרֶץ.

BLESSED ARE YOU, Adonai our God, Ruler of the Universe, who sanctified us by commanding us to eat matza.

Ba-ruch ata Adonai, Elo-hei-nu me-lech ha-olam, asher keed'sha-nu b'meetz-vo-tav v'tzee-va-nu al achee-lat matza.

בָּרוּךְ אַתָּה יְיָ, אֱלֹהֵינוּ מֶלֶךְ
הָעוֹלָם, אֲשֶׁר קִדְּשָׁנוּ בְּמִצְוֹתָיו
וְצִוָּנוּ עַל אֲכִילַת מַצָּה.

Maror

1. ***Take an ounce of raw maror,*** *preferably romaine lettuce, but almost equally good is horseradish ("chrein") which was popular in wintry northern Europe when lettuce was unavailable. Maror embodies the taste of slavery.*

2. ***Dip maror in charoset*** *(but not so much that it eradicates the bitter taste). Recite the blessing, eat and savor the maror, but **do not recline!** Reclining is a custom of the free, while maror and charoset remind us of persecution.*

HERE I AM, ready to perform the mitzvah of eating maror.

הִנְנִי מוּכָן וּמְזֻמָּן לְקַיֵּם מִצְוַת אֲכִילַת מָרוֹר.

BLESSED ARE YOU, Adonai our God, Ruler of the Universe who has sanctified us by commanding us to eat maror.

Ba-ruch ata Adonai, Elo-hei-nu me-lech Ha-olam, asher kee-d'sha-nu b'meetz-vo-tav v'tzee-va-nu al achee-lat maror.

בָּרוּךְ אַתָּה יְיָ אֱלֹהֵינוּ מֶלֶךְ הָעוֹלָם, אֲשֶׁר קִדְּשָׁנוּ בְּמִצְוֹתָיו וְצִוָּנוּ עַל אֲכִילַת מָרוֹר.

Kadesh

Urchatz

Karpas

Yachatz

Maggid

Rachtza

Motzi

Matza

Maror

Eating Bitter Herbs

Union Soldiers

ONE OF THE MOST literal yet inventive representations of charoset was conceived during the American Civil War, when a group of Jewish Union soldiers made a Seder for themselves in the wilderness of West Virginia. They had none of the ingredients for traditional charoset handy, so they put a real brick in its place on the Seder tray *(Ira Steingroot).*

"Charoset Taste Test"

Though neither the Torah nor Rabban Gamliel lists charoset with the essential "big three" – Pesach, matza and maror, it is still a mitzvah to eat charoset with the maror. In fact the rabbis were very explicit about its ingredients and their rationales.

Taste and compare two traditional recipes for charoset. Identify as many ingredients as possible. (See *Leader's Guide* p. 13)

Weeping Man

Ben Shahn ©
Ben Shahn/Vaga, NY

Sefer HaMinhagim, Amsterdam

The Blessing Over Chametz: Bergen-Belsen

BEFORE EATING CHAMETZ in the concentration camp Seder, Jews recited a special prayer:

"Our Father in Heaven! It is well-known to you that we desire to follow your will and celebrate Pesach with matza – strictly avoiding chametz. Yet our hearts are pained that the enslavement prevents us from doing so for our lives are in danger. We are here, ready to observe the positive commandment of **'living by your laws'** *(Lev. 18:5)* – not dying by them. We must take care not to violate the negative commandment, **'beware and guard yourself well,'** lest we endanger our lives. Therefore, our prayer to You is to preserve our lives and redeem us quickly, so that we may observe Your will and serve You wholeheartedly. Amen."

"Our Way" Passover brochure in sign language for the Jewish deaf (National Conference of Synagogue Youth of the Union of Orthodox Jewish Congregations of America).

Korech
Hillel's Sandwich at the Temple
followed by **Shulchan Orech**
The Pesach Family Meal

כּוֹרֵךְ

שֻׁלְחָן עוֹרֵךְ

Kadesh
Urchatz
Karpas
Yachatz
Maggid
Rachtza
Motzi
Matza
Maror
Korech
Shulchan Orech
Tzafun

Hillel's Sandwich and the Family Meal

Afikoman

Take the third, bottom matza, and prepare a sandwich of matza, maror and charoset. Eat it while reclining to the left. **Afterwards**, continue with the festive meal which concludes by eating the Afikoman as dessert.

Leader:
WE have just eaten matza and maror separately. However, in the days of the Temple, Hillel, the head of the Sanhedrin, used to bind into one sandwich: Pesach lamb, matza and maror. He ate them all together in order to observe the law: *"You shall eat it (the Pesach sacrifice) on matzot and maror"* (Numbers 9:11).

Eating the sandwich tonight reminds us of the way life combines moments of suffering (*maror*) and of relief (*matza*), enslavement and freedom.

All:
IN MEMORY of Pesach in the Temple as Hillel used to celebrate it.

זֵכֶר לְמִקְדָּשׁ כְּהִלֵּל.
כֵּן עָשָׂה הִלֵּל בִּזְמַן שֶׁבֵּית הַמִּקְדָּשׁ הָיָה
קַיָּם. הָיָה כּוֹרֵךְ פֶּסַח מַצָּה וּמָרוֹר וְאוֹכֵל
בְּיַחַד. לְקַיֵּם מַה שֶּׁנֶּאֱמַר (במדבר ט, יא):
"עַל מַצּוֹת וּמְרוֹרִים יֹאכְלֻהוּ."

A Soviet Sandwich

We held the Seder in a hurry, as in the time of the Exodus from Egypt, since the camp authorities prohibited the holding of a Seder. Instead of *maror*, we ate slices of onion, and for *zeroa* (roasted bone symbolizing the Passover sacrifice), we used burnt soup cubes. We read from one Haggadah, the only copy we had, and when we reached *korech*, we had nothing to put between the matzot. Then Joseph Mendelevich said, **"We do not need a symbol of our suffering. We have real suffering and we shall put that between the matzot."**

(Shimon Grillius, a prisoner in a Soviet labor camp, whose crime was his desire to make aliyah).

An English Sandwich

BRITISH NOBILITY gave us the word **"sandwich"** invented by John Montague, nicknamed "Jemmy Twitcher," an inveterate gambler in the court of George III. Famous for his round-the-clock sessions at the gaming tables, "Jemmy" used to order his servant to bring him pieces of meat between slices of bread, so that he could continue gambling without loss of time. Soon the bread-and-meat combination was called the **sandwich**. "Jemmy," you see, was more formally known as the fourth **Earl of Sandwich**. Sandwiches both during the Exodus in the 13th century B.C.E. and in 18th century England were **"fast foods."** In the twentieth century the revivers of the Hebrew language sat down to invent a term for the sandwich. They first suggested it be called a *"Hilleleet,"* named after Hillel, head of the Sanhedrin, just as the English "sandwich" was named after an illustrious personage. Later they settled for *"kareech"* from the verb that describes Hillel's original sandwich – *"Korech."* Today most Israelis call it a *"sandwich,"* a term borrowed from the English.

Eating the Hidden Afikoman

צָפוּן

1. **The Afikoman**, the other half of the middle matza which was hidden at the beginning of the Seder, must now be eaten. Its taste lingers as the last food eaten at the Seder.

2. **At this point** the leaders of the Seder "discover to their dismay" that the afikoman has been "stolen" by the children. Knowing that it must be eaten at the end of the meal, the leaders must bargain for its return.

3. **It is recommended** that Jewish prizes be offered (a book, a game) as well as the promise of some money. Some families ask the children to give 10% of their afikoman prize to a **Tzedaka** of their choice and to announce the beneficiary at this point. The adults may be solicited for matching gifts.

Meditation: Seeking Our Lost Other Half

Pesach is a holiday celebrating our reunion with the lost parts of ourselves. Often hiding and separating are essential stages in our life. On Seder night we hide and then seek the afikoman, reuniting the two parts separated at the beginning of the Seder. May we learn to discover the lost parts of ourselves, to become reconciled with relatives who have become distant and to find wholeness in a Jewish tradition from which we have become alienated. May the Divine Face, which is sometimes hidden, shine upon us.

Find the hidden Pesach Fours: 4 matzot, 4 presents, 4"?," 4 cups!

Tanya Zion

הִנְנִי מוּכָן וּמְזֻמָּן לְקַיֵּם מִצְוַת אֲכִילַת אֲפִיקוֹמָן זֵכֶר לְקָרְבַּן פֶּסַח הַנֶּאֱכָל עַל הַשּׂוֹבַע.

HERE I AM, ready to fulfill the mitzvah of eating the afikoman. This matza is a reminder of the Pesach sacrifice which was eaten on a full stomach in the days of the Temple!

Birkat Hamazon – Barech
The Blessing after the Meal

1. **After the meal** we thank God not only for the food but for all the Divine gifts we have received. These blessings are recited over the third cup of wine which we pour now and drink at the end of Birkat Hamazon (p. 67).

2. **Usually a guest** is chosen to lead the blessing, so that one can thank the hosts and God simultaneously. For three or more adults (post bar-mitzvah) the **invitation** is said (p. 65). For ten or more, add to the invitation the word "Eloheinu," our God, since God's presence dwells in community.

HERE I AM, ready to perform the mitzvah of thanking God for the food we have eaten. Just as it says, *"you shall eat and be satisfied and bless Adonai your God, for the good land God gave you"* (Deut. 8:10).

הִנְנִי מוּכָן וּמְזֻמָּן לְקַיֵּם מִצְוַת
עֲשֵׂה כְּמוֹ שֶׁכָּתוּב בַּתּוֹרָה:
"וְאָכַלְתָּ וְשָׂבַעְתָּ וּבֵרַכְתָּ."

A SONG OF ASCENTS
The Dream of the Return from Exile

they who sow in tears...
הַזֹּרְעִים בְּדִמְעָה

שִׁיר הַמַּעֲלוֹת

WHEN ADONAI restores the fortunes of Zion
– we see it as in a dream –
our mouths shall be filled with laughter,
our tongues, with songs of joy.
    Then shall they say among the nations,
    "Adonai has done great things for them!"
    Adonai will do great things for us
    and we shall rejoice.
Restore our fortunes, Adonai,
like watercourses in the Negev.
    They who sow in tears
    shall reap with songs of joy.
Though he goes along weeping,
carrying the seed-bag, he shall come back with
songs of joy, carrying his sheaves (Psalm 126).

Sheer ha–ma–alot.
B'shuv Adonai et sheev–at Tzion,
ha-yeenu k'chol-meem.
Az y'ma-lei s'chok pee-nu
u'l-sho–nei–nu reena,
Az yo-m'ru va–goyim
heeg–deel Adonai la–asot eem eleh.
Heeg–deel Adonai la–asot eemanu
ha–yee–nu s'mei-cheem.
Shuva Adonai, et sh'vee–tei-nu ka–afee–keem
ba–negev.
Ha–zor–eem b'deem–ah, b'reena yeek–tzo-ru.
Ha–loch yei–lech u–va–cho
no–sei me–shech hazara,
Bo yavo v'ree–na, no–sei alu–mo-tav.

בְּשׁוּב יְיָ אֶת שִׁיבַת צִיּוֹן
הָיִינוּ כְּחֹלְמִים.
אָז יִמָּלֵא שְׂחוֹק פִּינוּ
וּלְשׁוֹנֵנוּ רִנָּה
אָז יֹאמְרוּ בַגּוֹיִם,
הִגְדִּיל יְיָ לַעֲשׂוֹת עִם אֵלֶּה.
הִגְדִּיל יְיָ לַעֲשׂוֹת עִמָּנוּ
הָיִינוּ שְׂמֵחִים.
שׁוּבָה יְיָ אֶת שְׁבִיתֵנוּ
כַּאֲפִיקִים בַּנֶּגֶב.
הַזֹּרְעִים בְּדִמְעָה
בְּרִנָּה יִקְצֹרוּ.
הָלוֹךְ יֵלֵךְ וּבָכֹה
נֹשֵׂא מֶשֶׁךְ הַזָּרַע
בֹּא יָבֹא בְרִנָּה נֹשֵׂא אֲלֻמֹּתָיו.

Kadesh
Urchatz
Karpas
Yachatz
Maggid
Rachtza
Motzi
Matza
Maror
Korech
Shulchan Orech
Tzafun
Barech
Blessing after Eating

THE INVITATION

בִּרְכַּת הַמָּזוֹן

Leader *(raises the cup and begins):* My friends, let us bless God for the meal.

Cha-vei-rai n'va-rech.

חֲבֵרַי נְבָרֵךְ!

All: "May Adonai's name be blessed from now and forever" *(Psalm 113:2).*

Y'hee sheim Adonai m'vo-rach mei-ata v'ad olam.

יְהִי שֵׁם יְיָ מְבֹרָךְ מֵעַתָּה וְעַד עוֹלָם.

Leader *(repeats):* "May Adonai's name be blessed from now and forever."

Y'hee sheim Adonai m'vo-rach mei-ata v'ad olam.

יְהִי שֵׁם יְיָ מְבֹרָךְ מֵעַתָּה וְעַד עוֹלָם.

Leader *(adds words in parenthesis when there is a minyan):* With your permission, let us bless (our God) from whose food we have eaten.

Beer-shoot, n'va-rech (Eloheinu) she-achal-nu mee-shelo.

בִּרְשׁוּת מָרָנָן וְרַבָּנָן וְרַבּוֹתַי, נְבָרֵךְ (אֱלֹהֵינוּ) שֶׁאָכַלְנוּ מִשֶּׁלּוֹ.

All: Blessed be (our God) from whose food we have eaten.

Ba-ruch (Eloheinu) she-achal-nu mee-shelo, uv'tu-vo cha-yeenu.

בָּרוּךְ (אֱלֹהֵינוּ) שֶׁאָכַלְנוּ מִשֶּׁלּוֹ וּבְטוּבוֹ חָיִינוּ.

Leader *(repeats):* Blessed be (our God) from whose food we have eaten.

Ba-ruch (Eloheinu) she-achal-nu mee-shelo, uv'tu-vo cha-yeenu.

בָּרוּךְ (אֱלֹהֵינוּ) שֶׁאָכַלְנוּ מִשֶּׁלּוֹ וּבְטוּבוֹ חָיִינוּ.

All: Blessed be God, Blessed be the Divine Name.

Ba-ruch hu u-varuch sh'mo.

בָּרוּךְ הוּא וּבָרוּךְ שְׁמוֹ.

FIRST BLESSING: FOR THE FOOD
(traditionally attributed to Moshe)

BLESSED ARE YOU, Adonai our God, Ruler of the universe, who nourishes the whole world. Your kindness endures forever. May we never be in want of food, for God provides for all the creatures which God has created. **Blessed are You, Adonai, who feeds all.**

...will reap with joy!
...בְּרִעָה יִקְצֹרוּ!

Ba-ruch ata Adonai Elo-hei-nu
me-lech ha-olam,
Ha-zan et ha-olam ku-lo b'tuvo,
b'chen, b'chesed, u-v'ra-cha-meem
Hu no-ten le-chem l'chol ba-sar,
kee- l'olam chas-do,
Uv-tu-vo ha-gadol, ta-meed lo chasar lanu,
v'al yech-sar lanu ma-zon, l'olam va-ed,
Ba-avur she-mo ha-gadol,
kee-hu Eil zan um-far-neis la-kol
U-mei-teev la-kol, u-mei-cheen ma-zon
l'chol bree-yo-tav asher ba-ra,
Baruch ata Adonai, ha-zan et ha-kol.

בָּרוּךְ אַתָּה יְיָ, אֱלֹהֵינוּ
מֶלֶךְ הָעוֹלָם,
הַזָּן אֶת הָעוֹלָם כֻּלּוֹ בְּטוּבוֹ
בְּחֵן בְּחֶסֶד וּבְרַחֲמִים
הוּא נוֹתֵן לֶחֶם לְכָל בָּשָׂר
כִּי לְעוֹלָם חַסְדּוֹ.
וּבְטוּבוֹ הַגָּדוֹל תָּמִיד לֹא חָסַר לָנוּ,
וְאַל יֶחְסַר לָנוּ מָזוֹן לְעוֹלָם וָעֶד.
בַּעֲבוּר שְׁמוֹ הַגָּדוֹל,
כִּי הוּא אֵל זָן וּמְפַרְנֵס לַכֹּל
וּמֵטִיב לַכֹּל, וּמֵכִין מָזוֹן
לְכֹל בְּרִיּוֹתָיו אֲשֶׁר בָּרָא.
בָּרוּךְ אַתָּה יְיָ, הַזָּן אֶת הַכֹּל.

אֱלֹהֵינוּ וֵאלֹהֵי אֲבוֹתֵינוּ, **יַעֲלֶה וְיָבֹא**, וְיַגִּיעַ, וְיֵרָאֶה, וְיֵרָצֶה, וְיִשָּׁמַע, וְיִפָּקֵד, וְיִזָּכֵר זִכְרוֹנֵנוּ וּפִקְדוֹנֵנוּ, וְזִכְרוֹן אֲבוֹתֵינוּ, וְזִכְרוֹן מָשִׁיחַ בֶּן דָּוִד עַבְדֶּךָ, וְזִכְרוֹן יְרוּשָׁלַיִם עִיר קָדְשֶׁךָ, וְזִכְרוֹן כָּל עַמְּךָ בֵּית יִשְׂרָאֵל לְפָנֶיךָ, לִפְלֵיטָה לְטוֹבָה לְחֵן וּלְחֶסֶד וּלְרַחֲמִים, לְחַיִּים וּלְשָׁלוֹם **בְּיוֹם חַג הַמַּצּוֹת הַזֶּה.** זָכְרֵנוּ יְיָ אֱלֹהֵינוּ בּוֹ לְטוֹבָה. וּפָקְדֵנוּ בּוֹ לִבְרָכָה. וְהוֹשִׁיעֵנוּ בוֹ לְחַיִּים, וּבִדְבַר יְשׁוּעָה וְרַחֲמִים, חוּס וְחָנֵּנוּ, וְרַחֵם עָלֵינוּ וְהוֹשִׁיעֵנוּ, כִּי אֵלֶיךָ עֵינֵינוּ, כִּי אֵל מֶלֶךְ חַנּוּן וְרַחוּם אָתָּה.

וּבְנֵה יְרוּשָׁלַיִם עִיר הַקֹּדֶשׁ בִּמְהֵרָה בְיָמֵינוּ. **בָּרוּךְ אַתָּה יְיָ, בּוֹנֵה בְרַחֲמָיו יְרוּשָׁלָיִם, אָמֵן.**

FOURTH BLESSING:
FOR DIVINE GOODNESS
(added after the defeat of the Bar Kochba Revolt 135 C.E.)

בָּרוּךְ אַתָּה יְיָ אֱלֹהֵינוּ מֶלֶךְ הָעוֹלָם, הָאֵל אָבִינוּ, מַלְכֵּנוּ, אַדִּירֵנוּ בּוֹרְאֵנוּ, גּוֹאֲלֵנוּ, יוֹצְרֵנוּ, קְדוֹשֵׁנוּ קְדוֹשׁ יַעֲקֹב, רוֹעֵנוּ רוֹעֵה יִשְׂרָאֵל. הַמֶּלֶךְ הַטּוֹב, וְהַמֵּטִיב לַכֹּל, שֶׁבְּכָל יוֹם וָיוֹם הוּא הֵטִיב, הוּא מֵטִיב, הוּא יֵיטִיב לָנוּ. הוּא גְמָלָנוּ, הוּא גוֹמְלֵנוּ, הוּא יִגְמְלֵנוּ לָעַד לְחֵן וּלְחֶסֶד וּלְרַחֲמִים וּלְרֶוַח הַצָּלָה וְהַצְלָחָה בְּרָכָה וִישׁוּעָה נֶחָמָה, פַּרְנָסָה וְכַלְכָּלָה, וְרַחֲמִים, וְחַיִּים וְשָׁלוֹם, וְכָל טוֹב, וּמִכָּל טוּב לְעוֹלָם אַל יְחַסְּרֵנוּ.

הָרַחֲמָן, הוּא יִמְלוֹךְ עָלֵינוּ לְעוֹלָם וָעֶד.

הָרַחֲמָן, הוּא יִתְבָּרַךְ בַּשָּׁמַיִם וּבָאָרֶץ.

הָרַחֲמָן, הוּא יִשְׁתַּבַּח לְדוֹר דּוֹרִים, וְיִתְפָּאַר בָּנוּ לָעַד וּלְנֵצַח נְצָחִים, וְיִתְהַדַּר בָּנוּ לָעַד וּלְעוֹלְמֵי עוֹלָמִים.

הָרַחֲמָן, הוּא יְפַרְנְסֵנוּ בְּכָבוֹד.

הָרַחֲמָן, הוּא יִשְׁבּוֹר עֻלֵּנוּ מֵעַל צַוָּארֵנוּ וְהוּא יוֹלִיכֵנוּ קוֹמְמִיּוּת לְאַרְצֵנוּ.

הָרַחֲמָן, הוּא יִשְׁלַח לָנוּ בְּרָכָה מְרֻבָּה בַּבַּיִת הַזֶּה, וְעַל שֻׁלְחָן זֶה שֶׁאָכַלְנוּ עָלָיו.

SECOND BLESSING:
FOR THE LAND AND THE FOOD
(attributed to Joshua)

נוֹדֶה לְּךָ יְיָ אֱלֹהֵינוּ עַל שֶׁהִנְחַלְתָּ לַאֲבוֹתֵינוּ, אֶרֶץ חֶמְדָּה טוֹבָה וּרְחָבָה, וְעַל שֶׁהוֹצֵאתָנוּ יְיָ אֱלֹהֵינוּ מֵאֶרֶץ מִצְרַיִם, וּפְדִיתָנוּ, מִבֵּית עֲבָדִים, וְעַל בְּרִיתְךָ שֶׁחָתַמְתָּ בִּבְשָׂרֵנוּ, וְעַל תּוֹרָתְךָ שֶׁלִּמַּדְתָּנוּ, וְעַל חֻקֶּיךָ שֶׁהוֹדַעְתָּנוּ וְעַל חַיִּים חֵן וָחֶסֶד שֶׁחוֹנַנְתָּנוּ, וְעַל אֲכִילַת מָזוֹן שָׁאַתָּה זָן וּמְפַרְנֵס אוֹתָנוּ תָּמִיד, בְּכָל יוֹם וּבְכָל עֵת וּבְכָל שָׁעָה.

וְעַל הַכֹּל יְיָ אֱלֹהֵינוּ אֲנַחְנוּ מוֹדִים לָךְ, וּמְבָרְכִים אוֹתָךְ, יִתְבָּרַךְ שִׁמְךָ בְּפִי כָּל חַי תָּמִיד לְעוֹלָם וָעֶד.

כַּכָּתוּב: "וְאָכַלְתָּ וְשָׂבָעְתָּ, וּבֵרַכְתָּ אֶת יְיָ אֱלֹהֶיךָ עַל הָאָרֶץ הַטֹּבָה אֲשֶׁר נָתַן לָךְ." **בָּרוּךְ אַתָּה יְיָ, עַל הָאָרֶץ וְעַל הַמָּזוֹן.**

THIRD BLESSING:
FOR JERUSALEM
(attributed to David)

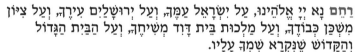

רַחֵם נָא יְיָ אֱלֹהֵינוּ, עַל יִשְׂרָאֵל עַמֶּךָ, וְעַל יְרוּשָׁלַיִם עִירֶךָ, וְעַל צִיּוֹן מִשְׁכַּן כְּבוֹדֶךָ, וְעַל מַלְכוּת בֵּית דָּוִד מְשִׁיחֶךָ, וְעַל הַבַּיִת הַגָּדוֹל וְהַקָּדוֹשׁ שֶׁנִּקְרָא שִׁמְךָ עָלָיו.

אֱלֹהֵינוּ, אָבִינוּ, רְעֵנוּ, זוּנֵנוּ, פַּרְנְסֵנוּ, וְכַלְכְּלֵנוּ, וְהַרְוִיחֵנוּ, וְהַרְוַח לָנוּ יְיָ אֱלֹהֵינוּ מְהֵרָה מִכָּל צָרוֹתֵינוּ. וְנָא, אַל תַּצְרִיכֵנוּ יְיָ אֱלֹהֵינוּ, לֹא לִידֵי מַתְּנַת בָּשָׂר וָדָם, וְלֹא לִידֵי הַלְוָאָתָם. כִּי אִם לְיָדְךָ הַמְּלֵאָה, הַפְּתוּחָה, הַקְּדוֹשָׁה וְהָרְחָבָה, שֶׁלֹּא נֵבוֹשׁ וְלֹא נִכָּלֵם לְעוֹלָם וָעֶד.

[On Shabbat add]:

רְצֵה וְהַחֲלִיצֵנוּ יְיָ אֱלֹהֵינוּ בְּמִצְוֹתֶיךָ וּבְמִצְוַת יוֹם הַשְּׁבִיעִי הַשַּׁבָּת הַגָּדוֹל וְהַקָּדוֹשׁ הַזֶּה. כִּי יוֹם זֶה גָּדוֹל וְקָדוֹשׁ הוּא לְפָנֶיךָ, לִשְׁבָּת בּוֹ וְלָנוּחַ בּוֹ בְּאַהֲבָה כְּמִצְוַת רְצוֹנֶךָ וּבִרְצוֹנְךָ הָנִיחַ לָנוּ יְיָ אֱלֹהֵינוּ, שֶׁלֹּא תְהֵא צָרָה וְיָגוֹן וַאֲנָחָה בְּיוֹם מְנוּחָתֵנוּ. וְהַרְאֵנוּ יְיָ אֱלֹהֵינוּ בְּנֶחָמַת צִיּוֹן עִירֶךָ, וּבְבִנְיַן יְרוּשָׁלַיִם עִיר קָדְשֶׁךָ, כִּי אַתָּה הוּא בַּעַל הַיְשׁוּעוֹת וּבַעַל הַנֶּחָמוֹת.

Kadesh
Urchatz
Karpas
Yachatz
Maggid
Rachtza
Motzi
Matza
Maror
Korech
Shulchan Orech
Tzafun
Barech

Blessing after Eating and Third Cup

הָרַחֲמָן, הוּא יִשְׁלַח לָנוּ אֶת אֵלִיָּהוּ הַנָּבִיא זָכוּר לַטּוֹב,
וִיבַשֶּׂר לָנוּ בְּשׂוֹרוֹת טוֹבוֹת יְשׁוּעוֹת וְנֶחָמוֹת.

הָרַחֲמָן, הוּא יְבָרֵךְ אֶת כָּל הַמְּסֻבִּין כָּאן אוֹתָנוּ וְאֶת כָּל אֲשֶׁר לָנוּ,
כְּמוֹ שֶׁנִּתְבָּרְכוּ אֲבוֹתֵינוּ, אַבְרָהָם יִצְחָק וְיַעֲקֹב. בַּכֹּל, מִכֹּל, כֹּל.
כֵּן יְבָרֵךְ אוֹתָנוּ כֻּלָּנוּ יַחַד בִּבְרָכָה שְׁלֵמָה, וְנֹאמַר אָמֵן.

בַּמָּרוֹם יְלַמְּדוּ עֲלֵיהֶם וְעָלֵינוּ זְכוּת, שֶׁתְּהֵא לְמִשְׁמֶרֶת שָׁלוֹם,
וְנִשָּׂא בְרָכָה מֵאֵת יְיָ וּצְדָקָה מֵאֱלֹהֵי יִשְׁעֵנוּ,
וְנִמְצָא חֵן וְשֵׂכֶל טוֹב בְּעֵינֵי אֱלֹהִים וְאָדָם.

[On Shabbat add]:

הָרַחֲמָן, הוּא יַנְחִילֵנוּ יוֹם שֶׁכֻּלּוֹ שַׁבָּת וּמְנוּחָה לְחַיֵּי הָעוֹלָמִים.

הָרַחֲמָן, הוּא יַנְחִילֵנוּ יוֹם שֶׁכֻּלּוֹ טוֹב.

הָרַחֲמָן, הוּא יְבָרֵךְ אֶת מְדִינַת יִשְׂרָאֵל.
הָרַחֲמָן, הוּא יַשְׁכִּין שָׁלוֹם בֵּין בְּנֵי יַעֲקֹב וּבְנֵי יִשְׁמָעֵאל.
הָרַחֲמָן, הוּא יְזַכֵּנוּ לִימוֹת הַמָּשִׁיחַ וּלְחַיֵּי הָעוֹלָם הַבָּא.

"מִגְדּוֹל יְשׁוּעוֹת מַלְכּוֹ, וְעֹשֶׂה חֶסֶד לִמְשִׁיחוֹ לְדָוִד וּלְזַרְעוֹ עַד עוֹלָם."
עֹשֶׂה שָׁלוֹם בִּמְרוֹמָיו, הוּא יַעֲשֶׂה שָׁלוֹם, עָלֵינוּ וְעַל כָּל יִשְׂרָאֵל,
וְאִמְרוּ אָמֵן.

"יְראוּ אֶת יְיָ קְדֹשָׁיו, כִּי אֵין מַחְסוֹר לִירֵאָיו. כְּפִירִים רָשׁוּ וְרָעֵבוּ,
וְדֹרְשֵׁי יְיָ לֹא יַחְסְרוּ כָל טוֹב. הוֹדוּ לַייָ כִּי טוֹב,
כִּי לְעוֹלָם חַסְדּוֹ. פּוֹתֵחַ אֶת יָדֶךָ, וּמַשְׂבִּיעַ לְכָל חַי רָצוֹן.
בָּרוּךְ הַגֶּבֶר אֲשֶׁר יִבְטַח בַּיְיָ, וְהָיָה יְיָ מִבְטַחוֹ."

"נַעַר הָיִיתִי גַּם זָקַנְתִּי וְלֹא רָאִיתִי צַדִּיק נֶעֱזָב,
וְזַרְעוֹ מְבַקֶּשׁ לָחֶם."
"יְיָ עֹז לְעַמּוֹ יִתֵּן, יְיָ יְבָרֵךְ אֶת עַמּוֹ בַשָּׁלוֹם."

TZEDAKA צדקה

The Third Cup

כּוֹס שְׁלִישִׁי

We conclude the Blessing over the Meal by drinking the Third Cup, the Cup of Blessing, while reclining to the left.

HERE I AM, ready to perform
the mitzvah of the third cup of wine,
which concludes this Pesach meal.

הִנְנִי מוּכָן וּמְזֻמָּן לְקַיֵּם
מִצְוַת כּוֹס שְׁלִישִׁי שֶׁל
אַרְבַּע כּוֹסוֹת.

BLESSED ARE YOU, Adonai
our God, Ruler of the Universe,
who creates the fruit of the vine.

*Ba-ruch ata Adonai
Elo-heinu me-lech ha-olam
bo-rei pree ha-gafen.*

בָּרוּךְ אַתָּה יְיָ,
אֱלֹהֵינוּ מֶלֶךְ הָעוֹלָם,
בּוֹרֵא פְּרִי הַגָּפֶן.

Cup of Elijah
and Pour Out Your Wrath

כּוֹס אֵלִיָּהוּ
שְׁפֹךְ חֲמָתְךָ

1. **Pour** a large cup of wine and open the door in honor of Elijah, who symbolizes future redemption. "He will reconcile the hearts of parents to their children and children to their parents." (Mal. 3:2-4)

2. **Stand and read** both the demand that our oppressors be brought to the bench of Divine justice, and the prayer for righteous Gentiles who rescued Jews.

Kadesh
Urchatz
Karpas
Yachatz
Maggid
Rachtza
Motzi
Matza
Maror
Korech
Shulchan Orech
Tzafun
Barech

Elijah's Cup

"Your Wrath" – A Late Addition

IT WAS NOT until the bloody Crusades that Biblical verses of Divine anger were added to the Haggadah, for pogroms typically occurred on Easter/Passover.

"Your Love" – A Later Addition

THIS UNIQUE addition to a medieval Haggadah appears side by side with "Pour out your wrath" in a manuscript from Worms (1521) attributed to the descendants of Rashi. Scholars today debate its authenticity but its sentiment for righteous gentiles is genuine.

"**POUR OUT** your fury
on the nations that do not know you,
upon the kingdoms
that do not invoke your name,
for they have devoured Jacob
and desolated his home" (Psalms 79:6,7).

"**POUR OUT** your wrath on them;
may your blazing anger overtake them" (Psalms 69:25).

"**PURSUE** them in wrath and destroy them
from under the heavens of Adonai!" (Lamentations 3:66).

"שְׁפֹךְ חֲמָתְךָ
אֶל הַגּוֹיִם, אֲשֶׁר לֹא יְדָעוּךָ
וְעַל מַמְלָכוֹת אֲשֶׁר
בְּשִׁמְךָ לֹא קָרָאוּ.
כִּי אָכַל אֶת יַעֲקֹב.
וְאֶת נָוֵהוּ הֵשַׁמּוּ."

"שְׁפָךְ עֲלֵיהֶם זַעְמֶךָ,
וַחֲרוֹן אַפְּךָ יַשִּׂיגֵם."

"תִּרְדֹּף בְּאַף וְתַשְׁמִידֵם,
מִתַּחַת שְׁמֵי יְיָ."

Pour Out Your Love
On Our Allies: Righteous Gentiles

"**POUR OUT** your love on the nations who have known you and on the kingdoms who call upon your name. For they show loving-kindness to the seed of Jacob and they defend your people Israel from those who would devour them alive. May they live to see the sukkah of peace spread over your chosen ones and to participate in the joy of your nations."

Anne Frank: I Still Believe

That's the difficulty in these times: ideals, dreams, and cherished hopes rise within us, only to meet the horrible truth and be shattered.

It's really a wonder that I haven't dropped all my ideals, because they seem so absurd and impossible to carry out. Yet I keep them, because in spite of everything I still believe that people are really good at heart. I simply can't build up my hopes on a foundation consisting of confusion, misery, and death. I see the world gradually being turned into a wilderness. I hear the ever-approaching thunder, which will destroy us, too. I can feel the suffering of millions – and yet, if I look up into the heavens, I think it will come out all right, that this cruelty too will end, and that peace and tranquillity will return again.

In the meantime, I must uphold my ideals, for perhaps the time will come when I shall be able to carry them out. *(Diary of Anne Frank, Amsterdam 1944)*

Opening the Door for Elijah   *Moritz Oppenheim (19th C. Germany)*

MESSIANIC SONGS OF HOPE

ELIJAH the prophet,
Elijah the Tishbee,
Elijah the Giladee.
May he soon come to us
Along with the Messiah, son of David.

Eliyahu ha-navee
Eliyahu ha-Tish-bee
Eliyahu ha-Giladee
beem-hei-ra b'ya-mei-nu
yavo ei-leinu eem ma-shee-ach ben David

אֵלִיָּהוּ הַנָּבִיא,
אֵלִיָּהוּ הַתִּשְׁבִּי,
אֵלִיָּהוּ הַגִּלְעָדִי.
בִּמְהֵרָה בְיָמֵנוּ, יָבוֹא אֵלֵינוּ
עִם מָשִׁיחַ בֶּן דָּוִד.

I BELIEVE with a perfect faith
in the coming of the Messiah
and even though he delays
I will await
the day of his coming.

Anee ma-a-meen b'eh-eh-mu-na
shlei-ma b'vee-at ha-ma-shee-ach
v'af-al-pee she-yeet-ma-mei-ah
eem kol zeh acha-keh lo
b'chol yom she-yavo

אֲנִי מַאֲמִין בֶּאֱמוּנָה
שְׁלֵמָה בְּבִיאַת הַמָּשִׁיחַ,
וְאַף עַל פִּי שֶׁיִּתְמַהְמֵהַּ,
עִם כָּל זֶה אֲחַכֶּה לוֹ
בְּכָל יוֹם שֶׁיָּבוֹא.

The Fourth Cup and the Festival Hallel

Ben Shahn, Hallelujah Suite
© Ben Shahn/Vaga

כּוֹס רְבִיעִי וְהַלֵּל

1. **The Pesach Seder** is divided into two parts by the meal itself. In fact, Hallel (Psalms 113-118) itself is split. While the first half of the Seder and of the Hallel (Psalms 113-114) is dedicated to the **past**, to historical memory of the redemption from Egypt, the second half looks forward to the **future** and ends with the wish: "Next year in Jerusalem!" Messianic hope inspires the singing from now to the completion of the Seder.

2. **Fill the fourth cup** of wine and place it before you and conclude singing the Festival Hallel.

לֹא לָנוּ יְיָ לֹא לָנוּ
כִּי לְשִׁמְךָ תֵּן כָּבוֹד, עַל חַסְדְּךָ עַל אֲמִתֶּךָ.
לָמָּה יֹאמְרוּ הַגּוֹיִם, אַיֵּה נָא אֱלֹהֵיהֶם.
וֵאלֹהֵינוּ בַשָּׁמָיִם כֹּל אֲשֶׁר חָפֵץ עָשָׂה.
עֲצַבֵּיהֶם כֶּסֶף וְזָהָב, מַעֲשֵׂה יְדֵי אָדָם.
פֶּה לָהֶם וְלֹא יְדַבֵּרוּ, עֵינַיִם לָהֶם וְלֹא יִרְאוּ.
אָזְנַיִם לָהֶם וְלֹא יִשְׁמָעוּ, אַף לָהֶם וְלֹא יְרִיחוּן.
יְדֵיהֶם וְלֹא יְמִישׁוּן, רַגְלֵיהֶם וְלֹא יְהַלֵּכוּ,
לֹא יֶהְגּוּ בִּגְרוֹנָם.
כְּמוֹהֶם יִהְיוּ עֹשֵׂיהֶם, כֹּל אֲשֶׁר בֹּטֵחַ בָּהֶם.
יִשְׂרָאֵל בְּטַח בַּייָ, עֶזְרָם וּמָגִנָּם הוּא.
בֵּית אַהֲרֹן בִּטְחוּ בַייָ, עֶזְרָם וּמָגִנָּם הוּא.
יִרְאֵי יְיָ בִּטְחוּ בַייָ, עֶזְרָם וּמָגִנָּם הוּא.

יְיָ זְכָרָנוּ יְבָרֵךְ,
יְבָרֵךְ אֶת בֵּית יִשְׂרָאֵל,
יְבָרֵךְ אֶת בֵּית אַהֲרֹן.
יְבָרֵךְ יִרְאֵי יְיָ, הַקְּטַנִּים עִם הַגְּדֹלִים.
יֹסֵף יְיָ עֲלֵיכֶם, עֲלֵיכֶם וְעַל בְּנֵיכֶם.
בְּרוּכִים אַתֶּם לַייָ, עֹשֵׂה שָׁמַיִם וָאָרֶץ.
הַשָּׁמַיִם שָׁמַיִם לַייָ, וְהָאָרֶץ נָתַן לִבְנֵי אָדָם.
לֹא הַמֵּתִים יְהַלְלוּ יָהּ, וְלֹא כָּל יֹרְדֵי דוּמָה.
וַאֲנַחְנוּ נְבָרֵךְ יָהּ, מֵעַתָּה וְעַד עוֹלָם, הַלְלוּיָהּ.

אָהַבְתִּי כִּי יִשְׁמַע יְיָ,
אֶת קוֹלִי תַּחֲנוּנָי.
כִּי הִטָּה אָזְנוֹ לִי וּבְיָמַי אֶקְרָא.
אֲפָפוּנִי חֶבְלֵי מָוֶת,
וּמְצָרֵי שְׁאוֹל מְצָאוּנִי
צָרָה וְיָגוֹן אֶמְצָא.
וּבְשֵׁם יְיָ אֶקְרָא,
אָנָּה יְיָ מַלְּטָה נַפְשִׁי.
חַנּוּן יְיָ וְצַדִּיק,
וֵאלֹהֵינוּ מְרַחֵם.
שֹׁמֵר פְּתָאיִם יְיָ
דַּלּוֹתִי וְלִי יְהוֹשִׁיעַ.
שׁוּבִי נַפְשִׁי לִמְנוּחָיְכִי,
כִּי יְיָ גָּמַל עָלָיְכִי.
כִּי חִלַּצְתָּ נַפְשִׁי מִמָּוֶת
אֶת עֵינִי מִן דִּמְעָה,
אֶת רַגְלִי מִדֶּחִי.
אֶתְהַלֵּךְ לִפְנֵי יְיָ,
בְּאַרְצוֹת הַחַיִּים.
הֶאֱמַנְתִּי כִּי אֲדַבֵּר,
אֲנִי עָנִיתִי מְאֹד.
אֲנִי אָמַרְתִּי בְחָפְזִי
כָּל הָאָדָם כֹּזֵב.

מָה אָשִׁיב לַייָ,
כָּל תַּגְמוּלוֹהִי עָלָי.
כּוֹס יְשׁוּעוֹת אֶשָּׂא,
וּבְשֵׁם יְיָ אֶקְרָא.
נְדָרַי לַייָ אֲשַׁלֵּם,
נֶגְדָה נָּא לְכָל עַמּוֹ.
יָקָר בְּעֵינֵי יְיָ הַמָּוְתָה לַחֲסִידָיו.
אָנָּה יְיָ כִּי אֲנִי עַבְדֶּךָ אֲנִי עַבְדְּךָ,
בֶּן אֲמָתֶךָ פִּתַּחְתָּ לְמוֹסֵרָי.
לְךָ אֶזְבַּח זֶבַח תּוֹדָה
וּבְשֵׁם יְיָ אֶקְרָא.
נְדָרַי לַייָ אֲשַׁלֵּם נֶגְדָה נָּא לְכָל עַמּוֹ.
בְּחַצְרוֹת בֵּית יְיָ בְּתוֹכֵכִי יְרוּשָׁלַיִם הַלְלוּיָהּ.

הַלְלוּ אֶת יְיָ,
כָּל גּוֹיִם,
שַׁבְּחוּהוּ כָּל הָאֻמִּים.
כִּי גָבַר עָלֵינוּ חַסְדּוֹ,
וֶאֱמֶת יְיָ לְעוֹלָם הַלְלוּיָהּ.

הוֹדוּ לַייָ כִּי טוֹב, כִּי לְעוֹלָם חַסְדּוֹ!
יֹאמַר נָא יִשְׂרָאֵל, כִּי לְעוֹלָם חַסְדּוֹ!
יֹאמְרוּ נָא בֵית אַהֲרֹן, כִּי לְעוֹלָם חַסְדּוֹ!
יֹאמְרוּ נָא יִרְאֵי יְיָ, כִּי לְעוֹלָם חַסְדּוֹ!

The Great Hallel   הַלֵּל הַגָּדוֹל

1. ***In addition to*** the usual Festival Hallel, on Seder night we add the Great Hallel
(Psalm 136). Both of them feature the famous refrain: כִּי לְעוֹלָם חַסְדּוֹ!

2. ***Some rabbis*** require or at least permit that an extra cup be drunk with the
Great Hallel. Some people dedicate this fifth cup to the reestablishment of the State
of Israel.

מִן הַמֵּצַר קָרָאתִי יָּהּ,
עָנָנִי בַמֶּרְחָב יָהּ.
יְיָ לִי לֹא אִירָא, מַה יַּעֲשֶׂה לִי אָדָם.
יְיָ לִי בְּעֹזְרָי, וַאֲנִי אֶרְאֶה בְשֹׂנְאָי.
טוֹב לַחֲסוֹת בַּיְיָ, מִבְּטֹחַ בָּאָדָם.
טוֹב לַחֲסוֹת בַּיְיָ מִבְּטֹחַ בִּנְדִיבִים.
כָּל גּוֹיִם סְבָבוּנִי
בְּשֵׁם יְיָ כִּי אֲמִילַם.
סַבּוּנִי גַם סְבָבוּנִי
בְּשֵׁם יְיָ כִּי אֲמִילַם.
סַבּוּנִי כִדְבֹרִים דֹּעֲכוּ כְּאֵשׁ קוֹצִים,
בְּשֵׁם יְיָ כִּי אֲמִילַם.
דָּחֹה דְחִיתַנִי לִנְפֹּל, וַיְיָ עֲזָרָנִי.
עָזִּי וְזִמְרָת יָהּ, וַיְהִי לִי לִישׁוּעָה.
קוֹל רִנָּה וִישׁוּעָה בְּאָהֳלֵי צַדִּיקִים,
יְמִין יְיָ עֹשָׂה חָיִל.
יְמִין יְיָ רוֹמֵמָה,
יְמִין יְיָ עֹשָׂה חָיִל.
לֹא אָמוּת כִּי אֶחְיֶה, וַאֲסַפֵּר מַעֲשֵׂי יָהּ.
יַסֹּר יִסְּרַנִּי יָּהּ, וְלַמָּוֶת לֹא נְתָנָנִי.

פִּתְחוּ לִי שַׁעֲרֵי צֶדֶק, אָבֹא בָם אוֹדֶה יָהּ.
זֶה הַשַּׁעַר לַיְיָ, צַדִּיקִים יָבֹאוּ בוֹ.

Ben Shahn, Hallelujah Suite
© Ben Shahn/Vaga

אוֹדְךָ כִּי עֲנִיתָנִי, וַתְּהִי לִי לִישׁוּעָה. (2x)
אֶבֶן מָאֲסוּ הַבּוֹנִים, הָיְתָה לְרֹאשׁ פִּנָּה. (2x)
מֵאֵת יְיָ הָיְתָה זֹּאת, הִיא נִפְלָאת בְּעֵינֵינוּ. (2x)
זֶה הַיּוֹם עָשָׂה יְיָ, נָגִילָה וְנִשְׂמְחָה בוֹ. (2x)

אָנָּא יְיָ הוֹשִׁיעָה נָּא! אָנָּא יְיָ הוֹשִׁיעָה נָּא!
אָנָּא יְיָ הַצְלִיחָה נָּא! אָנָּא יְיָ הַצְלִיחָה נָּא!

בָּרוּךְ הַבָּא בְּשֵׁם יְיָ, בֵּרַכְנוּכֶם מִבֵּית יְיָ. (2x)
אֵל יְיָ וַיָּאֶר לָנוּ, אִסְרוּ חַג בַּעֲבֹתִים, עַד קַרְנוֹת הַמִּזְבֵּחַ. (2x)
אֵלִי אַתָּה וְאוֹדֶךָּ אֱלֹהַי אֲרוֹמְמֶךָּ. (2x)
הוֹדוּ לַיְיָ כִּי טוֹב, כִּי לְעוֹלָם חַסְדּוֹ. (2x)

יְהַלְלוּךָ יְיָ אֱלֹהֵינוּ כָּל מַעֲשֶׂיךָ, וַחֲסִידֶיךָ צַדִּיקִים עוֹשֵׂי רְצוֹנֶךָ,
וְכָל עַמְּךָ בֵּית יִשְׂרָאֵל בְּרִנָּה יוֹדוּ וִיבָרְכוּ וִישַׁבְּחוּ וִיפָאֲרוּ וִירוֹמְמוּ
וְיַעֲרִיצוּ וְיַקְדִּישׁוּ וְיַמְלִיכוּ אֶת שִׁמְךָ מַלְכֵּנוּ, כִּי לְךָ טוֹב לְהוֹדוֹת
וּלְשִׁמְךָ נָאֶה לְזַמֵּר, כִּי מֵעוֹלָם וְעַד עוֹלָם אַתָּה אֵל.

כִּי לְעוֹלָם חַסְדּוֹ!	**הוֹדוּ לַיְיָ כִּי טוֹב,**
כִּי לְעוֹלָם חַסְדּוֹ!	הוֹדוּ לֵאלֹהֵי הָאֱלֹהִים,
כִּי לְעוֹלָם חַסְדּוֹ!	הוֹדוּ לַאֲדֹנֵי הָאֲדֹנִים,
כִּי לְעוֹלָם חַסְדּוֹ!	לְעֹשֵׂה נִפְלָאוֹת גְּדֹלוֹת לְבַדּוֹ,
כִּי לְעוֹלָם חַסְדּוֹ!	לְעֹשֵׂה הַשָּׁמַיִם בִּתְבוּנָה,
כִּי לְעוֹלָם חַסְדּוֹ!	לְרוֹקַע הָאָרֶץ עַל הַמָּיִם,
כִּי לְעוֹלָם חַסְדּוֹ!	לְעֹשֵׂה אוֹרִים גְּדֹלִים,
כִּי לְעוֹלָם חַסְדּוֹ!	אֶת הַשֶּׁמֶשׁ לְמֶמְשֶׁלֶת בַּיּוֹם,
כִּי לְעוֹלָם חַסְדּוֹ!	אֶת הַיָּרֵחַ וְכוֹכָבִים לְמֶמְשְׁלוֹת בַּלָּיְלָה,
כִּי לְעוֹלָם חַסְדּוֹ!	לְמַכֵּה מִצְרַיִם בִּבְכוֹרֵיהֶם,
כִּי לְעוֹלָם חַסְדּוֹ!	וַיּוֹצֵא יִשְׂרָאֵל מִתּוֹכָם,
כִּי לְעוֹלָם חַסְדּוֹ!	בְּיָד חֲזָקָה וּבִזְרוֹעַ נְטוּיָה,
כִּי לְעוֹלָם חַסְדּוֹ!	לְגֹזֵר יַם סוּף לִגְזָרִים,
כִּי לְעוֹלָם חַסְדּוֹ!	וְהֶעֱבִיר יִשְׂרָאֵל בְּתוֹכוֹ,
כִּי לְעוֹלָם חַסְדּוֹ!	וְנִעֵר פַּרְעֹה וְחֵילוֹ בְיַם סוּף,
כִּי לְעוֹלָם חַסְדּוֹ!	לְמוֹלִיךְ עַמּוֹ בַּמִּדְבָּר,
כִּי לְעוֹלָם חַסְדּוֹ!	לְמַכֵּה מְלָכִים גְּדֹלִים,
כִּי לְעוֹלָם חַסְדּוֹ!	וַיַּהֲרֹג מְלָכִים אַדִּירִים,
כִּי לְעוֹלָם חַסְדּוֹ!	לְסִיחוֹן מֶלֶךְ הָאֱמֹרִי,
כִּי לְעוֹלָם חַסְדּוֹ!	וּלְעוֹג מֶלֶךְ הַבָּשָׁן,
כִּי לְעוֹלָם חַסְדּוֹ!	וְנָתַן אַרְצָם לְנַחֲלָה,
כִּי לְעוֹלָם חַסְדּוֹ!	נַחֲלָה לְיִשְׂרָאֵל עַבְדּוֹ,
כִּי לְעוֹלָם חַסְדּוֹ!	שֶׁבְּשִׁפְלֵנוּ זָכַר לָנוּ,
כִּי לְעוֹלָם חַסְדּוֹ!	וַיִּפְרְקֵנוּ מִצָּרֵינוּ,
כִּי לְעוֹלָם חַסְדּוֹ!	נֹתֵן לֶחֶם לְכָל בָּשָׂר,
כִּי לְעוֹלָם חַסְדּוֹ!	הוֹדוּ לְאֵל הַשָּׁמָיִם,

The Blessing After the Hallel

נִשְׁמַת כָּל־חַי

Splitting the Red Sea

Joseph Horna, Mexico, 1946

נִשְׁמַת כָּל חַי, תְּבָרֵךְ אֶת שִׁמְךָ יְיָ אֱלֹהֵינוּ. וְרוּחַ כָּל בָּשָׂר, תְּפָאֵר וּתְרוֹמֵם זִכְרְךָ מַלְכֵּנוּ תָּמִיד, מִן הָעוֹלָם וְעַד הָעוֹלָם אַתָּה אֵל. וּמִבַּלְעָדֶיךָ אֵין לָנוּ מֶלֶךְ גּוֹאֵל וּמוֹשִׁיעַ, פּוֹדֶה וּמַצִּיל וּמְפַרְנֵס וּמְרַחֵם, בְּכָל עֵת צָרָה וְצוּקָה. אֵין לָנוּ מֶלֶךְ אֶלָּא אָתָּה: אֱלֹהֵי הָרִאשׁוֹנִים וְהָאַחֲרוֹנִים, אֱלוֹהַּ כָּל בְּרִיּוֹת, אֲדוֹן כָּל תּוֹלָדוֹת, הַמְהֻלָּל בְּרֹב הַתִּשְׁבָּחוֹת, הַמְנַהֵג עוֹלָמוֹ בְּחֶסֶד, וּבְרִיּוֹתָיו בְּרַחֲמִים. וַיְיָ לֹא יָנוּם וְלֹא יִישָׁן, הַמְעוֹרֵר יְשֵׁנִים וְהַמֵּקִיץ נִרְדָּמִים, וְהַמֵּשִׂיחַ אִלְּמִים, וְהַמַּתִּיר אֲסוּרִים, וְהַסּוֹמֵךְ נוֹפְלִים, וְהַזּוֹקֵף כְּפוּפִים, לְךָ לְבַדְּךָ אֲנַחְנוּ מוֹדִים. אִלּוּ פִינוּ מָלֵא שִׁירָה כַיָּם, וּלְשׁוֹנֵנוּ רִנָּה כַּהֲמוֹן גַּלָּיו, וְשִׂפְתוֹתֵינוּ שֶׁבַח כְּמֶרְחֲבֵי רָקִיעַ, וְעֵינֵינוּ מְאִירוֹת כַּשֶּׁמֶשׁ וְכַיָּרֵחַ, וְיָדֵינוּ פְרוּשׂוֹת כְּנִשְׁרֵי שָׁמָיִם, וְרַגְלֵינוּ קַלּוֹת כָּאַיָּלוֹת, אֵין אֲנַחְנוּ מַסְפִּיקִים, לְהוֹדוֹת לְךָ יְיָ אֱלֹהֵינוּ וֵאלֹהֵי אֲבוֹתֵינוּ, וּלְבָרֵךְ אֶת שְׁמֶךָ עַל אַחַת מֵאֶלֶף אֶלֶף אַלְפֵי אֲלָפִים וְרִבֵּי רְבָבוֹת פְּעָמִים, הַטּוֹבוֹת שֶׁעָשִׂיתָ עִם אֲבוֹתֵינוּ וְעִמָּנוּ.

מִמִּצְרַיִם גְּאַלְתָּנוּ יְיָ אֱלֹהֵינוּ, וּמִבֵּית עֲבָדִים פְּדִיתָנוּ, בְּרָעָב זַנְתָּנוּ, וּבְשָׂבָע כִּלְכַּלְתָּנוּ, מֵחֶרֶב הִצַּלְתָּנוּ, וּמִדֶּבֶר מִלַּטְתָּנוּ, וּמֵחֳלָיִם רָעִים וְנֶאֱמָנִים דִּלִּיתָנוּ.

עַד הֵנָּה עֲזָרוּנוּ רַחֲמֶיךָ, וְלֹא עֲזָבוּנוּ חֲסָדֶיךָ וְאַל תִּטְּשֵׁנוּ יְיָ אֱלֹהֵינוּ לָנֶצַח. עַל כֵּן אֵבָרִים שֶׁפִּלַּגְתָּ בָּנוּ, וְרוּחַ וּנְשָׁמָה שֶׁנָּפַחְתָּ בְּאַפֵּינוּ, וְלָשׁוֹן אֲשֶׁר שַׂמְתָּ בְּפִינוּ, הֵן הֵם יוֹדוּ וִיבָרְכוּ וִישַׁבְּחוּ וִיפָאֲרוּ וִירוֹמְמוּ וְיַעֲרִיצוּ וְיַקְדִּישׁוּ וְיַמְלִיכוּ אֶת שִׁמְךָ מַלְכֵּנוּ, כִּי כָל פֶּה לְךָ יוֹדֶה, וְכָל לָשׁוֹן לְךָ תִשָּׁבַע, וְכָל בֶּרֶךְ לְךָ תִכְרַע, וְכָל קוֹמָה לְפָנֶיךָ תִשְׁתַּחֲוֶה, וְכָל לְבָבוֹת יִירָאוּךָ, וְכָל קֶרֶב וּכְלָיוֹת יְזַמְּרוּ לִשְׁמֶךָ. כַּדָּבָר שֶׁכָּתוּב, כָּל עַצְמוֹתַי תֹּאמַרְנָה יְיָ מִי כָמוֹךָ. מַצִּיל עָנִי מֵחָזָק מִמֶּנּוּ, וְעָנִי וְאֶבְיוֹן מִגֹּזְלוֹ: מִי יִדְמֶה לָּךְ, וּמִי יִשְׁוֶה לָּךְ וּמִי יַעֲרָךְ לָךְ. הָאֵל הַגָּדוֹל הַגִּבּוֹר וְהַנּוֹרָא, אֵל עֶלְיוֹן קֹנֵה שָׁמַיִם וָאָרֶץ. נְהַלֶּלְךָ וּנְשַׁבֵּחֲךָ וּנְפָאֶרְךָ וּנְבָרֵךְ אֶת־שֵׁם קָדְשֶׁךָ. כָּאָמוּר, לְדָוִד, בָּרְכִי נַפְשִׁי אֶת יְיָ, וְכָל קְרָבַי אֶת שֵׁם קָדְשׁוֹ.

הָאֵל בְּתַעֲצֻמוֹת עֻזֶּךָ, הַגָּדוֹל בִּכְבוֹד שְׁמֶךָ. הַגִּבּוֹר לָנֶצַח וְהַנּוֹרָא בְּנוֹרְאוֹתֶיךָ. הַמֶּלֶךְ הַיּוֹשֵׁב עַל כִּסֵּא רָם וְנִשָּׂא.

שׁוֹכֵן עַד, מָרוֹם וְקָדוֹשׁ שְׁמוֹ: וְכָתוּב, רַנְּנוּ צַדִּיקִים בַּיְיָ, לַיְשָׁרִים נָאוָה תְהִלָּה. בְּפִי יְשָׁרִים תִּתְהַלָּל. וּבְדִבְרֵי צַדִּיקִים תִּתְבָּרַךְ. וּבִלְשׁוֹן חֲסִידִים תִּתְרוֹמָם. וּבְקֶרֶב קְדוֹשִׁים תִּתְקַדָּשׁ.

וּבְמַקְהֲלוֹת רִבְבוֹת עַמְּךָ בֵּית יִשְׂרָאֵל, בְּרִנָּה יִתְפָּאֵר שִׁמְךָ מַלְכֵּנוּ, בְּכָל דּוֹר וָדוֹר, שֶׁכֵּן חוֹבַת כָּל הַיְצוּרִים, לְפָנֶיךָ יְיָ אֱלֹהֵינוּ, וֵאלֹהֵי אֲבוֹתֵינוּ, לְהוֹדוֹת לְהַלֵּל לְשַׁבֵּחַ לְפָאֵר לְרוֹמֵם לְהַדֵּר לְבָרֵךְ לְעַלֵּה וּלְקַלֵּס, עַל כָּל דִּבְרֵי שִׁירוֹת וְתִשְׁבָּחוֹת דָּוִד בֶּן יִשַׁי עַבְדְּךָ מְשִׁיחֶךָ.

יִשְׁתַּבַּח שִׁמְךָ לָעַד מַלְכֵּנוּ, הָאֵל הַמֶּלֶךְ הַגָּדוֹל וְהַקָּדוֹשׁ בַּשָּׁמַיִם וּבָאָרֶץ. כִּי לְךָ נָאֶה, יְיָ אֱלֹהֵינוּ וֵאלֹהֵי אֲבוֹתֵינוּ: שִׁיר וּשְׁבָחָה, הַלֵּל וְזִמְרָה, עֹז וּמֶמְשָׁלָה, נֶצַח, גְּדֻלָּה וּגְבוּרָה, תְּהִלָּה וְתִפְאֶרֶת, קְדֻשָּׁה וּמַלְכוּת. בְּרָכוֹת וְהוֹדָאוֹת מֵעַתָּה וְעַד עוֹלָם.

בָּרוּךְ אַתָּה יְיָ, אֵל מֶלֶךְ גָּדוֹל בַּתִּשְׁבָּחוֹת, אֵל הַהוֹדָאוֹת, אֲדוֹן הַנִּפְלָאוֹת, הַבּוֹחֵר בְּשִׁירֵי זִמְרָה, מֶלֶךְ, אֵל, חֵי הָעוֹלָמִים.

The Fourth Cup

כּוֹס רְבִיעִי

Raise the fourth cup of wine, recite the blessing over it and recline to the left while drinking.

BLESSED ARE YOU, Adonai our God, Ruler of the Universe, who created the fruit of the vine.

Ba-ruch ata Adonai,
Elo-heinu me-lech ha-olam,
bo-rei pree ha-gafen.

בָּרוּךְ אַתָּה יְיָ,
אֱלֹהֵינוּ מֶלֶךְ הָעוֹלָם,
בּוֹרֵא פְּרִי הַגָּפֶן.

Blessing after Drinking Wine:

BLESSED ARE YOU, Adonai, for the vine and the fruit, for the beautiful and spacious land You gave us. Have mercy on us and bring us there to eat its fruits. Grant us happiness on this Feast of Matzot. Blessed are You, Adonai, for the land and for the fruit of the vine.

Ba-ruch ata Adonai al ha-aretz v'al pree ha-gafen.

בָּרוּךְ אַתָּה יְיָ אֱלֹהֵינוּ מֶלֶךְ הָעוֹלָם עַל הַגֶּפֶן וְעַל פְּרִי הַגֶּפֶן וְעַל
תְּנוּבַת הַשָּׂדֶה, וְעַל אֶרֶץ חֶמְדָּה טוֹבָה וּרְחָבָה, שֶׁרָצִיתָ וְהִנְחַלְתָּ
לַאֲבוֹתֵינוּ, לֶאֱכוֹל מִפִּרְיָהּ וְלִשְׂבּוֹעַ מִטּוּבָהּ. רַחֵם נָא יְיָ אֱלֹהֵינוּ עַל
יִשְׂרָאֵל עַמֶּךָ, וְעַל יְרוּשָׁלַיִם עִירֶךָ, וְעַל צִיּוֹן מִשְׁכַּן כְּבוֹדֶךָ, וְעַל מִזְבְּחֶךָ
וְעַל הֵיכָלֶךָ. וּבְנֵה יְרוּשָׁלַיִם עִיר הַקֹּדֶשׁ בִּמְהֵרָה בְיָמֵינוּ, וְהַעֲלֵנוּ
לְתוֹכָהּ, וְשַׂמְּחֵנוּ בְּבִנְיָנָהּ וְנֹאכַל מִפִּרְיָהּ וְנִשְׂבַּע מִטּוּבָהּ, וּנְבָרֶכְךָ עָלֶיהָ
בִּקְדֻשָּׁה וּבְטָהֳרָה (בשבת וּרְצֵה וְהַחֲלִיצֵנוּ בְּיוֹם הַשַּׁבָּת הַזֶּה) וְשַׂמְּחֵנוּ
בְּיוֹם חַג הַמַּצּוֹת הַזֶּה. כִּי אַתָּה יְיָ טוֹב וּמֵטִיב לַכֹּל, וְנוֹדֶה לְּךָ עַל
הָאָרֶץ וְעַל פְּרִי הַגָּפֶן. בָּרוּךְ אַתָּה יְיָ, עַל הָאָרֶץ וְעַל פְּרִי הַגָּפֶן.

On the second night of Pesach only:

Counting the Omer

סְפִירַת הָעֹמֶר

On the second night of Pesach we begin counting the 50 days from the Exodus to Sinai, from Pesach, the harvest of barley, until Shavuot, the harvest of wheat. We arrive at the giving of the Torah at Sinai and thus we move from freedom to responsibility.

Please rise and count off the first day of the Omer.

HERE I AM, ready to perform the mitzvah of counting the Omer.

הִנְנִי מוּכָן וּמְזֻמָּן לְקַיֵּם מִצְוַת
עֲשֵׂה שֶׁל סְפִירַת הָעֹמֶר.

BLESSED ARE YOU, Adonai our God, Ruler of the Universe, who has sanctified us with Divine laws and commanded us to count the Omer.

Ba-ruch ata Adonai, Elo-heinu me-lech ha-olam, asher keed'shanu b'meetz-vo-tav v'tzee-vanu al s'feerat ha-omer

בָּרוּךְ אַתָּה יְיָ אֱלֹהֵינוּ מֶלֶךְ
הָעוֹלָם, אֲשֶׁר קִדְּשָׁנוּ בְּמִצְוֹתָיו
וְצִוָּנוּ עַל סְפִירַת הָעֹמֶר.

TODAY is the first day of the Omer.

Ha-yom yom echad la-omer.

הַיּוֹם יוֹם אֶחָד לָעֹמֶר.

Kee Lo Naeh
It is Proper to Praise Him

This table song, by Jacob, a German poet, is an alphabetical acrostic praising God's many attributes. Though it has no connection to Pesach at all, it entered the Ashkenazi Haggadah after the 12th C. as a popular religious song.

The first verse typifies the style: "Mighty in royalty, Beautiful in stature, God's angels exclaim: To God alone belongs the Kingdom, for all this is becoming and fitting to God."

כִּי לוֹ נָאֶה

Refrain:

L'cha u-l'cha, l'cha kee l'cha, l'cha af l'cha.
L'cha Adonai ha-mam-lacha.
Kee lo na-eh, kee lo ya-eh.

אַדִּיר בִּמְלוּכָה, **בָּחוּר** כַּהֲלָכָה, **גְּדוּדָיו** יֹאמְרוּ לוֹ:
לְךָ וּלְךָ, לְךָ כִּי לְךָ, לְךָ אַף לְךָ,
לְךָ יְיָ הַמַּמְלָכָה.
כִּי לוֹ נָאֶה, כִּי לוֹ יָאֶה.

דָּגוּל בִּמְלוּכָה, **הָדוּר** כַּהֲלָכָה, **וָתִיקָיו** יֹאמְרוּ לוֹ:
לְךָ וּלְךָ, לְךָ כִּי לְךָ, לְךָ אַף לְךָ, לְךָ יְיָ הַמַּמְלָכָה.
כִּי לוֹ נָאֶה, כִּי לוֹ יָאֶה.

מוֹשֵׁל בִּמְלוּכָה, **נוֹרָא** כַּהֲלָכָה, **סְבִיבָיו** יֹאמְרוּ לוֹ:
לְךָ וּלְךָ, לְךָ כִּי לְךָ, לְךָ אַף לְךָ, לְךָ יְיָ הַמַּמְלָכָה.
כִּי לוֹ נָאֶה, כִּי לוֹ יָאֶה.

זַכַּאי בִּמְלוּכָה, **חָסִין** כַּהֲלָכָה, **טַפְסְרָיו** יֹאמְרוּ לוֹ:
לְךָ וּלְךָ, לְךָ כִּי לְךָ, לְךָ אַף לְךָ, לְךָ יְיָ הַמַּמְלָכָה.
כִּי לוֹ נָאֶה, כִּי לוֹ יָאֶה.

עָנָו בִּמְלוּכָה, **פּוֹדֶה** כַּהֲלָכָה, **צַדִּיקָיו** יֹאמְרוּ לוֹ:
לְךָ וּלְךָ, לְךָ כִּי לְךָ, לְךָ אַף לְךָ, לְךָ יְיָ הַמַּמְלָכָה.
כִּי לוֹ נָאֶה, כִּי לוֹ יָאֶה.

יָחִיד בִּמְלוּכָה, **כַּבִּיר** כַּהֲלָכָה, **לִמּוּדָיו** יֹאמְרוּ לוֹ:
לְךָ וּלְךָ, לְךָ כִּי לְךָ, לְךָ אַף לְךָ, לְךָ יְיָ הַמַּמְלָכָה.
כִּי לוֹ נָאֶה, כִּי לוֹ יָאֶה.

קָדוֹשׁ בִּמְלוּכָה, **רַחוּם** כַּהֲלָכָה, **שִׁנְאַנָּיו** יֹאמְרוּ לוֹ:
לְךָ וּלְךָ, לְךָ כִּי לְךָ, לְךָ אַף לְךָ, לְךָ יְיָ הַמַּמְלָכָה.
כִּי לוֹ נָאֶה, כִּי לוֹ יָאֶה.

תַּקִּיף בִּמְלוּכָה, **תּוֹמֵךְ** כַּהֲלָכָה, **תְּמִימָיו** יֹאמְרוּ לוֹ:
לְךָ וּלְךָ, לְךָ כִּי לְךָ, לְךָ אַף לְךָ, לְךָ יְיָ הַמַּמְלָכָה.
כִּי לוֹ נָאֶה, כִּי לוֹ יָאֶה.

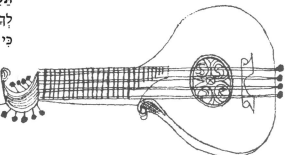

Adeer Hu
Mighty is God

אַדִּיר הוּא

The poet (15th C. Germany) recounts the Divine attributes in alphabetical order. and prays for the building of the third Temple.

*A*deer hu, adeer hu

Refrain: Yeev-neh veito b'ka-rov,
beem-hei-ra, beem-hei-ra,
B'ya-mei-nu b'ka-rov, Eil b'nei,
Eil b'nei, B'nei veit-cha b'ka-rov.

*B*a-chur hu, *g*a-dol hu, *d*a-gul hu,
Yeev-neh vei-to b'ka-rov . . .

*H*a-dur hu, *v*a-teek hu, *z*a-kai hu,
Yeev-neh vei-to b'ka-rov . . .

*C*ha-sid hu, *t*a-hor hu, *y*a-cheed hu,
Yeev-neh vei-to b'ka-rov . . .

*K*a-beer hu, *l*a-mud hu, *m*e-lech hu,
Yeev-neh vei-to b'ka-rov . . .

*N*o-ra hu, *s*a-geev hu, *ee*-zuz hu,
Yeev-neh vei-to b'ka-rov . . .

*P*o-deh hu, *tz*a-deek hu, *k*a-dosh hu,
Yeev-neh vei-to b'ka-rov . . .

*R*a-chum hu, *sh*a-dai hu, *t*a-keef hu,
Yeev-neh vei-to b'ka-rov . . .

אַדִּיר הוּא, אַדִּיר הוּא,

יִבְנֶה בֵיתוֹ בְּקָרוֹב,
בִּמְהֵרָה בִּמְהֵרָה, בְּיָמֵינוּ בְּקָרוֹב.
אֵל בְּנֵה, אֵל בְּנֵה, בְּנֵה בֵיתְךָ בְּקָרוֹב.

בָּחוּר הוּא, גָּדוֹל הוּא, דָּגוּל הוּא,
יִבְנֶה בֵיתוֹ בְּקָרוֹב . . .

הָדוּר הוּא, וָתִיק הוּא, זַכַּאי הוּא,
יִבְנֶה בֵיתוֹ בְּקָרוֹב . . .

חָסִיד הוּא, טָהוֹר הוּא, יָחִיד הוּא,
יִבְנֶה בֵיתוֹ בְּקָרוֹב . . .

כַּבִּיר הוּא, לָמוּד הוּא, מֶלֶךְ הוּא,
יִבְנֶה בֵיתוֹ בְּקָרוֹב . . .

נוֹרָא הוּא, סַגִּיב הוּא, עִזּוּז הוּא,
יִבְנֶה בֵיתוֹ בְּקָרוֹב . . .

פּוֹדֶה הוּא, צַדִּיק הוּא, קָדוֹשׁ הוּא,
יִבְנֶה בֵיתוֹ בְּקָרוֹב . . .

רַחוּם הוּא, שַׁדַּי הוּא, תַּקִּיף הוּא,
יִבְנֶה בֵיתוֹ בְּקָרוֹב . . .

Echad Mee Yodei-a
WHO KNOWS ONE?

אֶחָד מִי יוֹדֵעַ?

"Who knows one?" is modelled on a German non-Jewish folksong (15th or 16th C.).
It consists of a numerical quiz written like a basic Jewish trivia game.

Kadesh
Urchatz
Karpas
Yachatz
Maggid
Rachtza
Motzi
Matza
Maror
Korech
Shulchan Orech
Tzafun
Barech
Hallel
Nirtza

Who Knows One

 are the Fathers.

Shlo-sha mee yo-dei-a?
Shlo-sha anee yo-dei-a.
Shlo-sha avot,
Shnei lu-chot ha-breet,
Echad Elo-hei-nu
she-ba-sha-ma-yeem uva-aretz.

שְׁלֹשָׁה מִי יוֹדֵעַ?
שְׁלֹשָׁה אֲנִי יוֹדֵעַ!
שְׁלֹשָׁה אָבוֹת,
שְׁנֵי לֻחוֹת הַבְּרִית,
אֶחָד אֱלֹהֵינוּ
שֶׁבַּשָּׁמַיִם וּבָאָרֶץ.

 is our God, who is in heaven and on earth.

ECHAD MEE YO-DEI-A?
Echad anee yo-dei-a.
Echad Elo-hei-nu
she-ba-sha-ma-yeem uva-aretz.

אֶחָד מִי יוֹדֵעַ?
אֶחָד אֲנִי יוֹדֵעַ!
אֶחָד אֱלֹהֵינוּ
שֶׁבַּשָּׁמַיִם וּבָאָרֶץ.

 are the tablets of the Covenant.

Shna-yeem mee yo-dei-a?
Shna-yeem anee yo-dei-a.
Shnei lu-chot ha-breet,
Echad Elo-hei-nu
she-ba-sha-ma-yeem uva-aretz.

שְׁנַיִם מִי יוֹדֵעַ?
שְׁנַיִם אֲנִי יוֹדֵעַ!
שְׁנֵי לֻחוֹת הַבְּרִית,
אֶחָד אֱלֹהֵינוּ
שֶׁבַּשָּׁמַיִם וּבָאָרֶץ.

are the Mothers.

Arba mee yo-dei-a?
Arba anee yo-dei-a.
Arba eema-hot,
Shlo-sha avot,
Shnei lu-chot ha-breet,
Echad Elo-hei-nu
she-ba-sha-ma-yeem uva-aretz.

אַרְבַּע מִי יוֹדֵעַ?
אַרְבַּע אֲנִי יוֹדֵעַ!
אַרְבַּע אִמָּהוֹת,
שְׁלֹשָׁה אָבוֹת,
שְׁנֵי לֻחוֹת הַבְּרִית,
אֶחָד אֱלֹהֵינוּ
שֶׁבַּשָּׁמַיִם וּבָאָרֶץ.

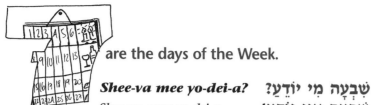 are the days of the Week.

Shee-va mee yo-dei-a? שִׁבְעָה מִי יוֹדֵעַ?

Shee-va anee yo-dei-a. שִׁבְעָה אֲנִי יוֹדֵעַ!

Shee-va y'mei Shab-ta, שִׁבְעָה יְמֵי שַׁבַּתָּא,

Shee-sha seedrei Mishna, שִׁשָּׁה סִדְרֵי מִשְׁנָה,

Cha-meesha chum-shei Torah, חֲמִשָּׁה חוּמְשֵׁי תוֹרָה,

Arba eema-hot, אַרְבַּע אִמָּהוֹת,

Shlo-sha avot, שְׁלֹשָׁה אָבוֹת,

Shnei lu-chot ha-breet, שְׁנֵי לֻחוֹת הַבְּרִית,

Echad Elo-hei-nu אֶחָד אֱלֹהֵינוּ

she-ba-sha-ma-yeem uva-aretz. שֶׁבַּשָּׁמַיִם וּבָאָרֶץ.

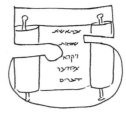 are the books of the Torah.

Cha-mee-sha mee yo-dei-a? חֲמִשָּׁה מִי יוֹדֵעַ?

Cha-mee-sha anee yo-dei-a. חֲמִשָּׁה אֲנִי יוֹדֵעַ!

Cha-mee-sha chum-shei Torah, חֲמִשָּׁה חוּמְשֵׁי תוֹרָה,

Arba eema-hot, אַרְבַּע אִמָּהוֹת,

Shlo-sha avot, שְׁלֹשָׁה אָבוֹת,

Shnei lu-chot ha-breet, שְׁנֵי לֻחוֹת הַבְּרִית,

Echad Elo-hei-nu אֶחָד אֱלֹהֵינוּ

she-ba-sha-ma-yeem uva-aretz. שֶׁבַּשָּׁמַיִם וּבָאָרֶץ.

 are the days before Circumcision.

Shmona mee yo-dei-a? שְׁמוֹנָה מִי יוֹדֵעַ?

Shmona anee yo-dei-a. שְׁמוֹנָה אֲנִי יוֹדֵעַ!

Shmona y'mei mee-la, שְׁמוֹנָה יְמֵי מִילָה,

Shee-va y'mei Shab-ta, שִׁבְעָה יְמֵי שַׁבַּתָּא,

Shee-sha seedrei Mishna, שִׁשָּׁה סִדְרֵי מִשְׁנָה,

Cha-meesha chum-shei Torah, חֲמִשָּׁה חוּמְשֵׁי תוֹרָה,

Arba eema-hot, אַרְבַּע אִמָּהוֹת,

Shlo-sha avot, שְׁלֹשָׁה אָבוֹת,

Shnei lu-chot ha-breet, שְׁנֵי לֻחוֹת הַבְּרִית,

Echad Elo-hei-nu אֶחָד אֱלֹהֵינוּ

she-ba-sha-ma-yeem uva-aretz. שֶׁבַּשָּׁמַיִם וּבָאָרֶץ.

 are the Mishna sections.

Shee-sha mee yo-dei-a? שִׁשָּׁה מִי יוֹדֵעַ?

Shee-sha anee yo-dei-a. שִׁשָּׁה אֲנִי יוֹדֵעַ!

Shee-sha seedrei Mishna, שִׁשָּׁה סִדְרֵי מִשְׁנָה,

Cha-meesha chum-shei Torah, חֲמִשָּׁה חוּמְשֵׁי תוֹרָה,

Arba eema-hot, אַרְבַּע אִמָּהוֹת,

Shlo-sha avot, שְׁלֹשָׁה אָבוֹת,

Shnei lu-chot ha-breet, שְׁנֵי לֻחוֹת הַבְּרִית,

Echad Elo-hei-nu אֶחָד אֱלֹהֵינוּ

she-ba-sha-ma-yeem uva-aretz. שֶׁבַּשָּׁמַיִם וּבָאָרֶץ.

Shee-sha see-drei Mishna,
Cha-mee-sha chum-shei Torah,
Arba eema-hot,
Shlo-sha avot,
Shnei lu-chot ha-breet,
Echad Elo-hei-nu
she-ba-sha-ma-yeem uva-aretz.

שִׁשָּׁה סִדְרֵי מִשְׁנָה,
חֲמִשָּׁה חֻמְשֵׁי תוֹרָה,
אַרְבַּע אִמָּהוֹת,
שְׁלֹשָׁה אָבוֹת,
שְׁנֵי לֻחוֹת הַבְּרִית,
אֶחָד אֱלֹהֵינוּ
שֶׁבַּשָּׁמַיִם וּבָאָרֶץ.

are the months of Pregnancy.

Tee-sha mee yo-dei-a?
Tee-sha anee yo-dei-a.
Tee-sha yar-chei lei-da,
Shmona y'mei mee-la,
Shee-va y'mei Shab-ta,
Shee-sha see-drei Mishna,
Cha-mee-sha chum-shei Torah,
Arba eema-hot,
Shlo-sha avot,
Shnei lu-chot ha-breet,
Echad Elo-hei-nu
she-ba-sha-ma-yeem uva-aretz.

תִּשְׁעָה מִי יוֹדֵעַ?
תִּשְׁעָה אֲנִי יוֹדֵעַ!
תִּשְׁעָה יַרְחֵי לֵדָה,
שְׁמוֹנָה יְמֵי מִילָה,
שִׁבְעָה יְמֵי שַׁבַּתָּא,
שִׁשָּׁה סִדְרֵי מִשְׁנָה,
חֲמִשָּׁה חֻמְשֵׁי תוֹרָה,
אַרְבַּע אִמָּהוֹת,
שְׁלֹשָׁה אָבוֹת,
שְׁנֵי לֻחוֹת הַבְּרִית,
אֶחָד אֱלֹהֵינוּ
שֶׁבַּשָּׁמַיִם וּבָאָרֶץ.

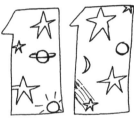

are the stars in Joseph's dream.

Echad-asar mee yo-dei-a?
Echad-asar anee yo-dei-a.
Echad-asar koch-va-ya,
A-sa-ra dee-bra-ya,
Tee-sha yar-chei lei-da,
Shmona y'mei mee-la,
Shee-va y'mei Shab-ta,
Shee-sha see-drei Mishna,
Cha-mee-sha chum-shei Torah,
Arba eema-hot,
Shlo-sha avot,
Shnei lu-chot ha-breet,
Echad Elo-hei-nu
she-ba-sha-ma-yeem uva-aretz.

אַחַד עָשָׂר מִי יוֹדֵעַ?
אַחַד עָשָׂר אֲנִי יוֹדֵעַ!
אַחַד עָשָׂר כּוֹכְבַיָּא,
עֲשָׂרָה דִבְּרַיָּא,
תִּשְׁעָה יַרְחֵי לֵדָה,
שְׁמוֹנָה יְמֵי מִילָה,
שִׁבְעָה יְמֵי שַׁבַּתָּא,
שִׁשָּׁה סִדְרֵי מִשְׁנָה,
חֲמִשָּׁה חֻמְשֵׁי תוֹרָה,
אַרְבַּע אִמָּהוֹת,
שְׁלֹשָׁה אָבוֹת,
שְׁנֵי לֻחוֹת הַבְּרִית,
אֶחָד אֱלֹהֵינוּ
שֶׁבַּשָּׁמַיִם וּבָאָרֶץ.

are the Ten Commandments.

A-sa-ra mee yo-dei-a?
A-sa-ra anee yo-dei-a.
A-sa-ra dee-bra-ya,
Tee-sha yar-chei lei-da,
Shmona y'mei mee-la,
Shee-va y'mei Shab-ta,

עֲשָׂרָה מִי יוֹדֵעַ?
עֲשָׂרָה אֲנִי יוֹדֵעַ!
עֲשָׂרָה דִבְּרַיָּא,
תִּשְׁעָה יַרְחֵי לֵדָה,
שְׁמוֹנָה יְמֵי מִילָה,
שִׁבְעָה יְמֵי שַׁבַּתָּא,

Kadesh
Urchatz
Karpas
Yachatz
Maggid
Rachtza
Motzi
Matza
Maror
Korech
Shulchan Orech
Tzafun
Barech
Hallel
Nirtza

Who Knows One

 are God's attributes of mercy.

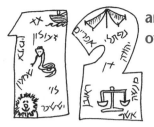 are the Tribes of Israel.

Shlo-sha-asar mee yo-dei-a?	שְׁלֹשָׁה עָשָׂר מִי יוֹדֵעַ?
Shlo-sha-asar anee yo-dei-a.	שְׁלֹשָׁה עָשָׂר אֲנִי יוֹדֵעַ!
Shlo-sha-asar mee-da-ya,	שְׁלֹשָׁה עָשָׂר מִדַּיָּא,
Shneim-asar sheev-ta-ya,	שְׁנֵים עָשָׂר שִׁבְטַיָּא,
Echad-asar koch-va-ya,	אַחַד עָשָׂר כּוֹכְבַיָּא,
A-sa-ra dee-bra-ya,	עֲשָׂרָה דִּבְּרַיָּא,
Tee-sha yar-chei lei-da,	תִּשְׁעָה יַרְחֵי לֵדָה,
Shmona y'mei mee-la,	שְׁמוֹנָה יְמֵי מִילָה,
Shee-va y'mei Shab-ta,	שִׁבְעָה יְמֵי שַׁבַּתָּא,
Shee-sha see-drei Mishna,	שִׁשָּׁה סִדְרֵי מִשְׁנָה,
Cha-mee-sha chum-shei Torah,	חֲמִשָּׁה חוּמְשֵׁי תוֹרָה,
Arba eema-hot,	אַרְבַּע אִמָּהוֹת,
Shlo-sha avot,	שְׁלֹשָׁה אָבוֹת,
Shnei lu-chot ha-breet,	שְׁנֵי לֻחוֹת הַבְּרִית,
Echad Elo-hei-nu	אֶחָד אֱלֹהֵינוּ
she-ba-sha-ma-yeem uva-aretz.	שֶׁבַּשָּׁמַיִם וּבָאָרֶץ.

Shneim-asar mee yo-dei-a?	שְׁנֵים עָשָׂר מִי יוֹדֵעַ?
Shneim-asar anee yo-dei-a.	שְׁנֵים עָשָׂר אֲנִי יוֹדֵעַ!
Shneim-asar sheev-ta-ya,	שְׁנֵים עָשָׂר שִׁבְטַיָּא,
Echad-asar koch-va-ya,	אַחַד עָשָׂר כּוֹכְבַיָּא,
A-sa-ra dee-bra-ya,	עֲשָׂרָה דִּבְּרַיָּא,
Tee-sha yar-chei lei-da,	תִּשְׁעָה יַרְחֵי לֵדָה,
Shmona y'mei mee-la,	שְׁמוֹנָה יְמֵי מִילָה,
Shee-va y'mei Shab-ta,	שִׁבְעָה יְמֵי שַׁבַּתָּא,
Shee-sha see-drei Mishna,	שִׁשָּׁה סִדְרֵי מִשְׁנָה,
Cha-mee-sha chum-shei Torah,	חֲמִשָּׁה חוּמְשֵׁי תוֹרָה,
Arba eema-hot,	אַרְבַּע אִמָּהוֹת,
Shlo-sha avot,	שְׁלֹשָׁה אָבוֹת,
Shnei lu-chot ha-breet,	שְׁנֵי לֻחוֹת הַבְּרִית,
Echad Elo-hei-nu	אֶחָד אֱלֹהֵינוּ
she-ba-sha-ma-yeem uva-aretz.	שֶׁבַּשָּׁמַיִם וּבָאָרֶץ.

Singing Activity

Since the song is written in question and answer form, you may assign the answers to different participants. The whole "chorus" sings the question: **"Who knows one (two, etc.)?"** and the preassigned respondent sings the answer **"I know one, One is our God . . . "** every time that number comes up. No one dare fall asleep and miss a turn in the rotation.

An Advanced "Who Knows One?"

Who knows three? Name the three fathers of Israel. (Hint: A... , I..., J...)

Who knows the four mothers of the Torah? (Hint: S..., R..., R ..., L...)

Who knows the "fours" of the Seder?

Who knows the five books of the Torah in English and in Hebrew?
(Hint: G..., E..., L..., N..., D...; ...ד, ...ו, ...ו, ...ש, ...ב)

Who knows the ten commandments? (See Exodus 20)

Who knows the ten plagues?

*Who knows Jacob's twelve sons?** Hint: Leah's sons: R..., Sh..., L..., J..., Y..., Z...   Rachel's: J..., B...   Zilpah's: G..., A...   Bilhah's: D..., N...

Who knows 613?

Chad Gad-ya
Just One Kid

This is the Jewish *"Old MacDonald Had a Farm." Preassign a stanza to volunteers who must produce an appropriate sound or gesture for each subsequent aggressor. For example, the goat might say "maa," the cat "meow," and the dog "woof." The stick could make a banging sound, the fire might "sizzle," and the water, "glug-glug." Think up appropriate sounds for the ox and the slaughterer. The angel of death* *and God require the greatest creativity and delicacy. Everyone sings the verses, while the preassigned participant adds a sound and/or visual effect each time. For example, "ata shunra (meow) v'achla l'gad-ya (maa-maa) . . . " [The cat came (meow) and ate up the goat (maa-maa) that my Father bought for two coins].*

The song, translated below, appears in Hebrew on p. 82.

The song, translated below, appears in Hebrew on p. 82.

Chorus:
Just one kid, just one kid
That my Abba bought for two zuzeem.
CHAD GADYA, CHAD GADYA.

1 Along came the **cat** *("meow")*
   and ate the **kid** *("maa")*
   that my **Abba** bought for two zuzeem.
   CHAD GADYA, CHAD GADYA.

2 Along came the **dog** *("woof")*
   and bit the **cat** *("meow")*
   that ate the **kid** *("maa")*
   that my **Abba** bought for two zuzeem.
   CHAD GADYA, CHAD GADYA.

3 Along came the **stick** *("bang")*
   and hit the **dog** *("woof")* . . .

4 Along came the **fire** *("sizzle")*
   and burned the **stick** *("bang")* . . .

5 Along came the **water** *("gurgle")*
   and quenched the **fire** *("sizzle")* . . .

6 Along came the **ox** *("slurp")*
   and drank the **water** *("gurgle")* . . .

Final Verse:

9 Then came **the Holy One**, blessed be He
   and destroyed the **angel of death**
   that slew the **slaughterer**
   that killed the **ox** *("slurp")*
   that drank the **water** *("gurgle")*
   that quenched the **fire** *("sizzle, crackle")*
   that burned the **stick** *("bang")*
   that beat the **dog** *("woof")*
   that bit the **cat** *("meow")*
   that ate the **kid** *("maa")*
   that my **Abba** bought for two zuzeem.
   CHAD GADYA, CHAD GADYA.

Kadesh
Urchatz
Karpas
Yachatz
Maggid
Rachtza
Motzi
Matza
Maror
Korech
Shulchan Orech
Tzafun
Barech
Hallel
Nirtza

Chad Gadya

Measure for Measure

WRITTEN IN ARAMAIC and modelled on German folksongs, this ballad – which has no overt connection to Pesach – entered the Ashkenazi Haggadah in the 15th-16th century. Hardpressed Jewish commentators have discovered a moral lesson between the lines: measure for measure, an oppressor will always be swallowed by a greater oppressor until God redeems the world from death.

Slipping in a Popular Tune

ALTHOUGH THERE ARE ancient Jewish melodies, many "Jewish" melodies are originally borrowed from the general musical world. The Hassidic movement made it a great virtue to borrow secular tunes and redirect their musical energies to the service of God. For example, French Habad (Lubavitch) Hassidim enjoy singing Shabbat songs to the music of the *Marseillaise* – the secularist anthem of the French Revolution. They believe that thereby they are redeeming the divine sparks of creativity that have been imprisoned in the encasing of a misguided militantly anti-religious movement.

You too may wish to set the words of the Pesach songs to well-known showtunes or folksongs (for example, *"There was an old lady who swallowed a fly"*).

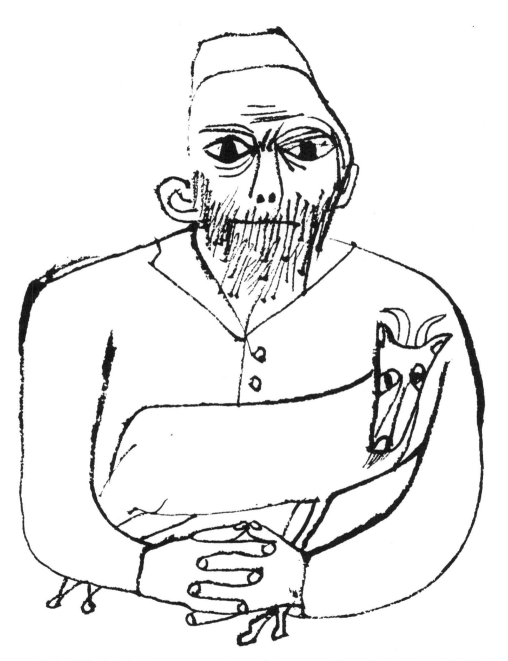

Ben Shahn, "Chad Gadya"

CHAD GAD-YA, CHAD GAD-YA

D'za-been abba bee-trei zu-zei
Chad gad-ya (2x)

חַד גַּדְיָא, חַד גַּדְיָא
דְּזַבִּין אַבָּא בִּתְרֵי זוּזֵי,
חַד גַּדְיָא, חַד גַּדְיָא.

V'ata shun-ra v'ach-la l'gad-ya
D'za-been abba bee-trei zu-zei
Chad gad-ya (2x)

וְאָתָא שׁוּנְרָא, וְאָכְלָה לְגַדְיָא,
דְּזַבִּין אַבָּא בִּתְרֵי זוּזֵי,
חַד גַּדְיָא, חַד גַּדְיָא.

V'ata chal-ba v'na-scha-ch l'shun-ra
D'ach-la l'gad-ya
D'za-been abba bee-trei zu-zei
Chad gad-ya (2x)

וְאָתָא כַלְבָּא, וְנָשַׁךְ לְשׁוּנְרָא,
דְּאָכְלָה לְגַדְיָא,
דְּזַבִּין אַבָּא בִּתְרֵי זוּזֵי,
חַד גַּדְיָא, חַד גַּדְיָא.

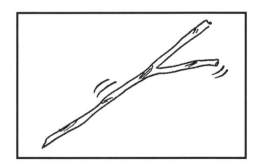

V'ata chu-tra v'hee-ka l'chal-ba
D'na-shach l'shun-ra
D'ach-la l'gad-ya
D'za-been abba bee-trei zu-zei
Chad gad-ya (2x)

וְאָתָא חוּטְרָא, וְהִכָּה לְכַלְבָּא,
דְּנָשַׁךְ לְשׁוּנְרָא, דְּאָכְלָה לְגַדְיָא,
דְּזַבִּין אַבָּא בִּתְרֵי זוּזֵי,
חַד גַּדְיָא, חַד גַּדְיָא.

V'ata nura v'saraf l'chu-tra
D'hee-ka l'chal-ba
D'na-shach l'shun-ra
D'ach-la l'gad-ya
D'za-been abba bee-trei zu-zei
Chad gad-ya (2x)

וְאָתָא נוּרָא, וְשָׂרַף לְחוּטְרָא,
דְּהִכָּה לְכַלְבָּא,
דְּנָשַׁךְ לְשׁוּנְרָא,
דְּאָכְלָה לְגַדְיָא,
דְּזַבִּין אַבָּא בִּתְרֵי זוּזֵי,
חַד גַּדְיָא, חַד גַּדְיָא.

V'ata maya v'cha-va l'nura
D'saraf l'chu-tra
D'hee-ka l'chal-ba
D'na-shach l'shun-ra
D'ach-la l'gad-ya
D'za-been abba bee-trei zu-zei
Chad gad-ya (2x)

וְאָתָא מַיָּא, וְכָבָה לְנוּרָא,
דְּשָׂרַף לְחוּטְרָא,
דְּהִכָּה לְכַלְבָּא,
דְּנָשַׁךְ לְשׁוּנְרָא,
דְּאָכְלָה לְגַדְיָא,
דְּזַבִּין אַבָּא בִּתְרֵי זוּזֵי,
חַד גַּדְיָא, חַד גַּדְיָא.

V'ata tora v'shata l'maya
D'chava l'nura
D'saraf l'chu-tra
D'hee-ka l'chal-ba
D'na-shach l'shun-ra
D'ach-la l'gad-ya
D'za-been abba bee-trei zu-zei
Chad gad-ya (2x)

וְאָתָא תוֹרָא, וְשָׁתָא לְמַיָּא,
דְּכָבָה לְנוּרָא,
דְּשָׂרַף לְחוּטְרָא,
דְּהִכָּה לְכַלְבָּא,
דְּנָשַׁךְ לְשׁוּנְרָא,
דְּאָכְלָה לְגַדְיָא,
דְּזַבִּין אַבָּא בִּתְרֵי זוּזֵי,
חַד גַּדְיָא, חַד גַּדְיָא.

V'ata ha-sho-cheit v'sha-chat l'tora
D'shata l'maya
D'chava l'nura
D'saraf l'chu-tra
D'hee-ka l'chal-ba
D'na-shach l'shunra
D'ach-la l'gad-ya
D'za-been abba bee-trei zu-zei
Chad gad-ya (2x)

וְאָתָא הַשּׁוֹחֵט, וְשָׁחַט לְתוֹרָא,
דְּשָׁתָא לְמַיָּא,
דְּכָבָה לְנוּרָא,
דְּשָׂרַף לְחוּטְרָא,
דְּהִכָּה לְכַלְבָּא,
דְּנָשַׁךְ לְשׁוּנְרָא,
דְּאָכְלָה לְגַדְיָא,
דְּזַבִּין אַבָּא בִּתְרֵי זוּזֵי,
חַד גַּדְיָא, חַד גַּדְיָא.

V'ata ma-lach ha-mavet
   v'sha-chat la-sho-cheit
D'sha-chat l'tora
D'shata l'maya
D'chava l'nura
D'saraf l'chu-tra
D'hee-ka l'chal-ba
D'na-shach l'shunra
D'ach-la l'gad-ya
D'za-been abba bee-trei zu-zei
Chad gad-ya (2x)

וְאָתָא מַלְאַךְ הַמָּוֶת, וְשָׁחַט לְשׁוֹחֵט,
דְּשָׁחַט לְתוֹרָא,
דְּשָׁתָא לְמַיָּא,
דְּכָבָה לְנוּרָא,
דְּשָׂרַף לְחוּטְרָא,
דְּהִכָּה לְכַלְבָּא,
דְּנָשַׁךְ לְשׁוּנְרָא,
דְּאָכְלָה לְגַדְיָא,
דְּזַבִּין אַבָּא בִּתְרֵי זוּזֵי,
חַד גַּדְיָא, חַד גַּדְיָא.

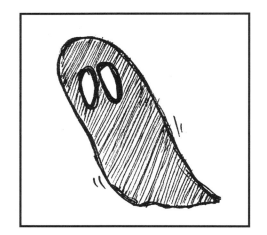

Arye Allweil
(first Israeli Army Haggadah, 1949)

V'ata Ha-Ka-dosh Baruch Hu
   v'sha-chat l'ma-lach ha-mavet
D'sha-chat la-sho-cheit
D'sha-chat l'tora
D'shata l'maya
D'chava l'nura
D'saraf l'chu-tra
D'hee-ka l'chal-ba
D'na-shach l'shunra
D'ach-la l'gad-ya
D'za-been abba bee-trei zu-zei
Chad gad-ya (2x)

וְאָתָא הַקָּדוֹשׁ בָּרוּךְ הוּא,
וְשָׁחַט לְמַלְאַךְ הַמָּוֶת,
דְּשָׁחַט לְשׁוֹחֵט,
דְּשָׁחַט לְתוֹרָא,
דְּשָׁתָא לְמַיָּא,
דְּכָבָה לְנוּרָא,
דְּשָׂרַף לְחוּטְרָא,
דְּהִכָּה לְכַלְבָּא,
דְּנָשַׁךְ לְשׁוּנְרָא,
דְּאָכְלָה לְגַדְיָא,
דְּזַבִּין אַבָּא בִּתְרֵי זוּזֵי,
חַד גַּדְיָא, חַד גַּדְיָא.

Kadesh
Urchatz
Karpas
Yachatz
Maggid
Rachtza
Motzi
Matza
Maror
Korech
Shulchan Orech
Tzafun
Barech
Hallel
Nirtza

Next
Year
in
Jerusalem

Conclusion - Nirtza

נִרְצָה

1. **The Pesach Seder** ends with a prayer that all our efforts to perform the Seder properly may be pleasing and acceptable to God. The prayer was composed by Rabbi Yosef Tov-Elem, 11th C. France.

2. **We also** look forward to next year's Seder. Hopefully we will celebrate it in a more peaceful world and in a fully restored Jerusalem. We conclude with **Next Year in Jerusalem.**

Oseh Shalom

GOD makes peace in heaven, and so may God make peace over us, all Israel [and humanity]. Amen.

עֹשֶׂה שָׁלוֹם בִּמְרוֹמָיו
הוּא יַעֲשֶׂה שָׁלוֹם עָלֵינוּ
וְעַל כָּל יִשְׂרָאֵל, וְאִמְרוּ אָמֵן.

Oseh shalom beem-romav
hu ya-aseh shalom aleinu
v'al kol Yisrael v'eemru amen.

The Concluding Poem: Looking Forward to Next Year's Seder

CONCLUDED is the Pesach Seder,
Finished down to the last detail
with all its laws and customs.
As we have been able to conduct this Seder,
So may we someday perform it in Jerusalem.
Pure One who dwells in the palace,
Support your congregation countless in number.
May you soon lead the offshoots of your stock,
Bringing the redeemed to Zion in joy.

חֲסַל סִדּוּר פֶּסַח כְּהִלְכָתוֹ,
כְּכָל מִשְׁפָּטוֹ וְחֻקָּתוֹ.
כַּאֲשֶׁר זָכִינוּ לְסַדֵּר אוֹתוֹ,
כֵּן נִזְכֶּה לַעֲשׂוֹתוֹ.

זָךְ שׁוֹכֵן מְעוֹנָה,
קוֹמֵם קְהַל עֲדַת מִי מָנָה.
בְּקָרוֹב נַהֵל נִטְעֵי כַנָּה,
פְּדוּיִם לְצִיּוֹן בְּרִנָּה.

Otto Geismar, 1927

All sing:

לְשָׁנָה הַבָּאָה בִּירוּשָׁלַיִם!
La-Shana Ha-ba-a Bee-Yeru-sha-layeem!
NEXT YEAR IN JERUSALEM!

Storyteller's Appendix

"The more one expands and embellishes the story, the more commendable it is"

כָּל הַמַּרְבֶּה

The Haggadah recommends that parents go beyond the text of the Haggadah and improvise dramatically in retelling the story of the Exodus. The **traditional Haggadah does not include a script for the storyteller** nor even bring the appropriate Biblical chapters.

Some parents like to tell the story in their own words. Others ask the children to retell what they have learned in school under three major headings:

1. What was it like to be a slave?
2. What do you know about Moshe as a baby and as a young man?
3. How did the Jews finally become free?

(Before the Seder ask the children to prepare drawings to illustrate these themes and then to show and tell what they drew).

   Many parents prefer to use a script. Try reading aloud one of the following selections (pages 86-90).

A Philosopher at Home: David Hartman

OUR FAMILY labors a long time at our Seder trying to grasp the first part of the Haggadah: *"We were slaves in the land of Egypt."* I ask my children: **What do you think it feels like to be a slave?**

ONCE I TOLD my four-year-old a story about a boy who did not see his Daddy for a year: "The boy had a birthday and Daddy couldn't come. Then Daddy called and said, 'I'm going to come home.' The boy invited all his friends to come and see his Daddy, because he loved him. He said, **'Abba is coming home.'** He watched his Mommy cook kugel, his Daddy's favorite. Just after his friends had come, Abba called to say, 'The boss won't let me come.' The little boy said, 'What do you mean, the boss won't let you come? Tell him your son wants you home. Everybody wants you. We miss you!'"

SUDDENLY I could not help it, I started crying and my son started crying about the kid in the story. I created this dialogue of the Abba trying to explain to his little son: "I can't make my own decisions. The boss decides my movements for me." We felt the loneliness of the little boy who wanted so much to see his father but who knew that his love is not enough to bring him home. **That is what it means to be a slave. You can't control your life.**

(That is the story I tell when my child is four. At twelve, I tell another story. At sixteen, still another. On Pesach night I am a multi-faceted storyteller because my autobiography encompasses so many dimensions).

Otto Geismar, 1927

"By Tomorrow Today Will Be a Story"

Isaac Bashevis Singer:

"When a day passes, it is no longer there. What remains of it? Nothing more than a story. If stories weren't told or books weren't written, humans would live like the beasts, only for the day."

Reb Zebulun said, "Today we live, but by tomorrow today will be a story. **The whole world, all human life, is one long story.**"

Children are as puzzled by passing time as grownups. What happens to a day once it is gone? Where are all our yesterdays with their joys and sorrows? Literature helps us remember the past with its many moods. **To the storyteller yesterday is still here** as are the years and the decades gone by.

In stories time does not vanish. Neither do people and animals. For the writer and his readers, all creatures go on living forever. What happened long ago is still present.

(I.B. Singer, Nobel prize laureate, Yiddish literature, from Zlateh the Goat)

Forgetfulness and Memory

"Forgetfulness leads to exile, while memory is the secret of redemption," says the Baal Shem Tov *(18th C. founder of Hassidism)*. Therefore, we celebrate Passover by teaching ourselves to become inventive storytellers and empathetic listeners.

Trieste Haggadah, 1864

Not By Bread Alone

In the spring of 1945 a father and his teenage son shared the harsh labor in the Nazi camp. The father suggested a pact between them to save part of what little bread they received. After several days of saving the father reported to his son sheepishly: "I am sorry but I have given away our whole store of bread to a new arrival." "Why?" asked the son in desperation. The father explained, "There are two reasons: First, he needed food even more than we and second, I exchanged the bread for a miniature Haggadah." Several days later using this Haggadah, the father was able to raise people's spirits by conducting a Seder for many inmates. Even though matza was unavailable, the Seder gave everyone a special kind of nourishment – hope.

Ben Shahn, "Weeping Man"
(© 1996 Ben Shahn/Vaga, NY)

Heroic Women and Baby Moses

retold by Diana Craig (The Young Moses)

In one small corner of Egypt, just where the great river Nile runs into the sea, there lived some people called Israelites. They had come from Israel to Egypt many years before to look for food.

God had promised to look after the Israelites in their new home, and at first everyone was very happy. There was plenty to eat, and they grew strong and had lots of children. Soon their families filled the land.

But then everything changed. The king of Egypt, who was called the Pharaoh, died, and a new Pharaoh became king. He hated the Jews.

"There are so many of them," he grumbled. "Just think what would happen if they turned against us. They might even take sides with our enemies. We must stop them!" So he thought of a plan. **"We'll make them our slaves,"** he announced with an evil grin. "We'll work them so hard they won't even have time to think of fighting us . . . with a bit of luck they may even die of exhaustion!"

So the Jews slaved from sunrise to sunset, making bricks and moving huge stones to build Egyptian cities. When they were not building cities, they had to dig the fields and plant all the wheat and barley.

The Jews were exhausted, just as the Pharaoh had hoped. But they didn't die. In fact, they didn't even get ill. They stayed just as strong and healthy as ever. The Pharaoh's wicked plan wasn't working.

So he had another idea. He told the nurses that they must kill all Israelite baby boys as soon as they were born. But the nurses knew that God would not approve if they did such a terrible thing, so they made up an excuse.

"We're so sorry, Your Majesty," they lied, not daring to look the Pharaoh in the eye. "But the babies are born so quickly that we never get there in time."

"All right then," replied the Pharaoh angrily. "They'll just have to be thrown in the river instead!"

All the Jewish mothers were terrified and tried to hide their babies. One mother hid her newborn boy in a corner of her house. If anyone heard him crying and wondered about the noise, she knew what to say.

"It's a sick sheep I'm looking after," she would tell them. "Funny, isn't it, how they sound just like babies when they're ill?" No one suspected anything.

Leon Baxter

But soon the baby grew too big to hide. "I know what I'll do," thought his mother. "I'll make a little ark of reeds and float the baby on the river, near where the Pharaoh's daughter comes to wash every morning, and she's sure to find him. She has no children of her own, and she's not nearly as cruel as that wicked king. Perhaps she'll feel sorry for my baby and save him."

So the mother took a big basket and painted the outside with black, sticky stuff called pitch, to stop the water from getting in. Then she laid the baby inside and put the basket among the reeds near the river bank. She told her daughter, Miriam, to stay and see what happened.

Sure enough, the princess came down to the water's edge and stopped the basket. She sent one of her servants to fetch it, and she was amazed to see a little baby tucked up snugly inside.

"Whatever are you doing here?" she exclaimed, picking him up and giving him a cuddle. And then she guessed the truth. "You must be one of the Jewish babies, and your mother has hidden you here for safety. Well, I don't care what my father says, I won't throw you in the river."

88

Returning Moses to the Haggadah

SOME HAVE ARGUED that Moses was deliberately excluded from the Haggadah to avoid deifying a human leader. Certainly the hero of the traditional Haggadah is and should be God. But it is likely that Moses was often mentioned in the rabbinic Seder when parents told their children the story of the Exodus. We have introduced Moses explicitly into our Haggadah as recommended by Moses Maimonides: *"It is a mitzvah to tell the children about the Exodus even if they did not ask . . . If the children are mature and wise, tell them all that happened to us in Egypt and all the miracles God did for us by means of Moses . . . ."*
(Laws of Chametz and Matza 7:2).

Who Will Be Today's Midwives?

ONE SUNDAY morning in 1941 in Nazi-occupied Netherlands, a mysterious character rode up on his bicycle and entered the Calvinist Church. He ascended the podium and read aloud the story of the midwives who saved the Hebrew babies and defied Pharaoh's policy of genocide. "Who is today's Pharaoh?" he asked. "Hitler," the congregation replied. "Who are today's Hebrew babies?" "The Jews." "Who will be today's midwives?" He left the church, leaving his question hanging in the air.

During the war (1941-1945) seven families from this little church hid Jews and other resisters from the Nazis.

(See the full story in the Leader's Guide, p. 49)

Moses' Mother and Sister   Simon Solomon, England, 19th C.

The Shifra and Puah Award

AL AXELRAD, the Hillel rabbi at Brandeis University in the 1960's, established this annual award for non-violent resistance to tyranny. He named it after the midwives who resisted and outsmarted Pharoah and saved the Hebrew infants from drowning. (In Tel Aviv the maternity hospital is located at the intersection of Shifra and Puah Street).

To whom would you give this award this year?

Moses Comes of Age

retold by Diana Craig (The Flight from Egypt)

When the little boy was old enough, his mother took him back to the princess. "From now on, I shall be his mother," the princess said, "and I'll call him Moses, because I took him from the water." So Moses was brought up like an Egyptian prince, and had everything he could wish for.

But as the years went by, one thing began to bother Moses more and more. **Although he lived with the Egyptians, he knew he wasn't one of them.** He knew he was really a Jew. He saw how cruel the Egyptians were to his people and it made him very angry. How could the Egyptians treat them so badly? They hadn't done anything wrong. **It just wasn't fair.**

One day, when Moses had grown up, he decided to visit one of the building sites and see for himself what was going on. He caught sight of one of the Egyptian slave drivers beating a Hebrew slave. Moses completely lost his temper. He picked up a stone and smashed it on the slave driver's head. The man fell to the ground, dead. Moses was horrified at what he had done. Quickly, he buried the body in the sand.

"Don't breathe a word of what's happened, or the Pharaoh will have me killed!" he warned the slave. But the man just couldn't help telling his brother,

Leon Baxter

Leon Baxter

and his brother told his aunt, and his aunt told her friend . . . and soon everyone knew.

The next day, Moses visited another building site, and saw a big, strong slave bullying a small, weak slave.

"Stop that, you great bully!" shouted Moses.

"Just you try and make me!" the slave answered back cheekily. "You can't boss me about, or I'll tell the Pharaoh how you killed one of his men!"

Moses was terrified. His secret was out, and he knew that when the Pharaoh heard, that would be the end of him.

So, that night, he packed a few clothes and some food and, with a last, longing look at his home, he crept away.

Chronicles

News of the Past

15 Aviv 2524 © Reubeni Foundation

Dr. Israel Eldad & Moshe Aumann, Editors

WE QUIT EGYPT TODAY

Pharaoh gives in to Moses as 10th plague wipes out Kingdom's First-born.

Rameses, 15 Aviv. - Moses' oft-repeated plea to Pharaoh Merneptah, to "let my people go", was finally heard today, just after midnight, when the king of Egypt, badly shaken by the death of his eldest son, not only agreed to Moses' request, but actually insisted that the Israelites leave the country immediately. Pharaoh had sent for the Israelite leaders as soon as word had reached him that all of Egypt's first-born – including Pharaoh's – had been "mysteriously" struck down at midnight.

Moses and Aaron had expected the call. They had left for Rameses several hours earlier, after Moses had told reporters : "The period of haggling is over. This time we are going to tell Pharaoh briefly and precisely: Tonight we leave. And I think that this time Pharaoh will relent."

Pharaoh Capitulates

Merneptah surrounded by his Council of Magicians, addressed Moses and Aaron in these words:

"Rise up and get you forth from among my people – you and the Children of Israel – and go serve your Lord as you have said. Take your flocks and your herds and be gone!"

But then Merneptah began to mention terms and limitations.

To the consternation of those present, Moses dared to interrupt Pharaoh, as he curtly rejected all conditions. This was unprecedented in the palace, and contrary to the sacred protocol, in which Moses is well-versed.

Moses declared emphatically that he had been willing to discuss terms before God smote the land of Egypt – but not any more. A smitten people, he added, does not dictate terms; it has to accept them.

Sons of Jacob: Tribes of Israel!

This month shall be unto you the beginning of months. This day shall be unto you the first day of all days till the end of time. For today you have been delivered from slavery unto freedom. Today you have become a nation.

Egypt, with its taskmasters and its heathen beliefs, is behind you. In front of you is the desert, vast and terrible. But this terrifying wilderness leads to a land flowing with milk and honey, to the land of your fathers. Be not dismayed.

For if you will remain faithful to the covenant and willingly undertake all the sacrifices the Lord may exact from you – then He will allow no harm to come to you, and your enemy shall not overpower you.

As you have emerged today from bondage unto freedom, so shall you be free tomorrow in the land of your fathers.

Hear, O Israel: The Lord our God, the Lord is one!

MOSES, The Son of Amram

Hebrews Spared

A summary check of Israelite homes in the Goshen province reveals that the Angel of Death, on his way to smite the sons of Egypt, passed over the families of the Hebrews and left them intact.

It seems the Children of Israel were under God's special protection tonight, for not only are all the first-born sons still alive – but no Israelite died in the course of the night, even of so-called natural causes.

Permissions

We wish to thank all those who allowed us to use their creative work in this family Haggadah. We apologize to those whom we were unable to locate to request their permission and to offer them copyright fees.

1. **Yariv Ben Aharon**, *HaKibbutz*.
2. **Dick Codor**, "The Marx Brothers," *The Big Book of Jewish Humor*.
3. **Diana Craig** and **Leon Baxter**, *The Young Moses* and *The Flight from Egypt*, Mac Donald Co., London.
4. **Dr. Israel Eldad**, *Chronicles* and *Hegyonot Chazal* by permission of Batya Washitz, Reubeni Foundation and Moshe Aumann.
5. **Tully Filmus**, from the JPS book of his drawings.
6. **Paul Freeman**, **Nota Koslowsky** and **Siegmund Forst**, illustrations published by the Shulsinger Brothers.
7. **Otto Geismar**, by permission of his offspring.
8. **Tzvi Livni**, Yavneh Publishers.
9. **David Moss**, *The Moss Haggadah*, courtesy of Bet Alpha Editions, P.O.B. 20042, Rochester, N.Y. 14602 and by the generous permission of the artist.
10. **Henry Noerdlinger**, *Moses and Egypt*.
11. **Dov Noy**, *The Beautiful Girl and the Three Princes* (Hebrew, 1965) contains the Iraqi folktale, "Rags to Riches."
12. **Rony Oren**, figures from *The Animated Haggadah* by the generous permission of Scopus Films © Jonathan Lubell.
13. **Dan Reisinger**, *Feast of Freedom*, ed. Rachel Anne Rabinowicz, © Rabbinical Assembly of America 1982, Reprinted by permission.
14. **Ben Shahn** ©1996 Estate of Ben Shahn/Licensed by Vaga, NY, NY.
15. **Jakob Steinhardt**, **Moses Lilien**, **Joseph Horna** and **Arye Allweil** illustrations of the Haggadah.
16. **Arthur Szyk** by the generous permission of his daughter, Mrs. Alexandra Bracie.
17. **David Wander**, *The Haggadah in Memory of the Holocaust* (©1988, a artist's generous permission.
18. **Shraga Weil**, "Song of Songs" © 1968 Sifriat HaPoalim, by permission of the artist.
19. **I. B. Singer**, *Zlateh the Goat*, © 1966; and **Ira Steingroot**, *Keeping Passover*, © 1995, by permission of HarperCollins.

Sponsors

May God bless these sponsors for their generous support of this family Haggadah. For full sponsor list and dedications, see unabridged *A Different Night*, pp. 9-11.

Eunice and Ernest Benchell

Dr. Emile and Gail Bendit

Marilyn, Ellen and David Bierman

Deborah and Gerald Charnoff

Gary and Margey Cheses

Goldie and Sam Cohen

Ann and Ari Deshe

Leonard Fein

Rina and Samuel Frankel

Jean and Jerry Friedman

Susan and Michael Gelman

Herb and Dee Dee Glimcher

Gary and Cari Gross

Dr. Merle and Anna Hillman

LeRoy E. and Rebecca Hoffberger

Holly and Bradley Kastan

Elie Katz

Jodie Katz

The Kayne and Kane families

Brenda Brown-Lipitz

Philip and Phyllis Margolius

The children of Harvey and Lyn Meyerhoff

Bonnie and David Milenthal

The Family of David Moskowitz

Karen and Neil Moss

Henry and Bella Muller

Charles and Ilana Horowitz Ratner

Bernice Rosenthal

Leonard and Lainy LeBow Sachs

Marc Saltzberg

Jeffrey and Jodie Schein

Robert and Janice Schottenstein

Steven and Jill Schottenstein

Alvin Cramer Segal

Kathy Levin Shapiro and Sandy Shapiro

The Family of Hyman Shapiro

Chuck and Joyce Shenk

Charna Sherman

Marc Silverstein

Carol and Norman Traeger

The Wexner Heritage Fellows of Phoenix

Gordon and Carol Zacks